Raphaële Vidaling

ENCHANTING BOOK NOOKS

Miniature Worlds and Settings to Craft and Decorate

RIZZOLI UNIVERSE

CONTENTS

INTRODUCTION

> Miniatures are an exercise in metaphysical freshness; they allow for modification with little risk. And what a sense of peace in creating such a controlled world! Miniatures soothe without ever dulling the senses.
> In them, the imagination is alert and joyful.
>
> GASTON BACHELARD,
> *The Poetics of Space*

Just what is a book nook? It is a narrow space between books on a shelf where a three-dimensional miniature world unfolds. Though this recent trend originated in Japan, it has quickly spread to the Western world, where in many languages, the English term *book nook* has been adopted—short, rhyming, and evocative of the playful secrecy of this tiny world tucked between book spines.

A book nook reveals infinity in the in-between. It allows one to step into literature in a literal sense, as if pushing open a small door between the words to access the vastness of the imagination. Montesquieu once wrote, "When I want to unwind, I take my small microscopes and look at a lemon or a moth."

In a similar manner, makers worldwide have embraced the book nook format to illustrate scenes from their favorite works: dark alleyways from thrillers, enchanted forests from fairy tales, a magician's lair, or a Victorian library filled with mystery, all created to fit perfectly on the shelf where the box is inserted. A small model can just as easily slip between poetry collections or paperback novels, and who is to say a Lilliputian kitchen cannot be nestled among cookbooks?

The key elements of a book nook are its size—tall, narrow, and deep—and its miniaturization. In many ways, book nooks signal a revival of framed miniature displays, which were once popular but fell out of fashion. The concept is not new; it is a rightful heir to the dioramas invented in the nineteenth century by Louis Daguerre, the father of photography, who worked as a theater set designer. Originally, a diorama referred to a massive painted canvas illuminated through a system of moving glass panels that would simulate, for example, a sunset descending over a landscape. The technique was a sensation in its time, enough for Honoré de Balzac to call it "the wonder of the century."

Today, the word *diorama* more commonly refers to a re-creation of a realistic scene, whether life-size or miniature. Museums use dioramas for educational displays, and among hobbyists, they overlap with model making, particularly among model train and architecture enthusiasts.

The decorative miniature wall displays that were once in vogue created the illusion of an alcove, as if the wall concealed hidden wonders beyond its surface. Book nooks, embedded within bookshelves, take this illusion even further. Their depth adds an element of mystery that catches the eye, which is further captivated by clever lighting. What is happening in that sliver of light calling out to me?

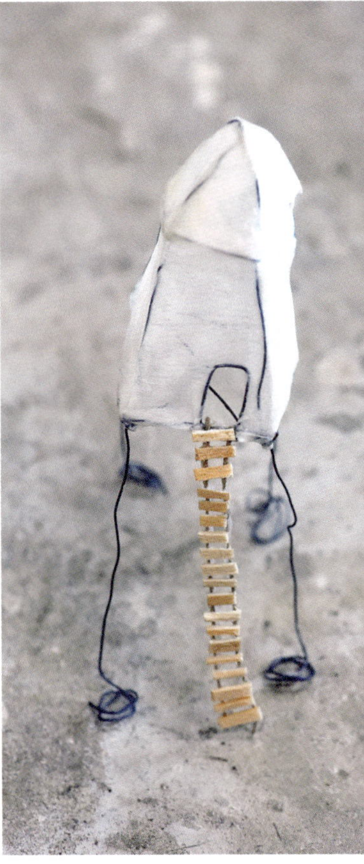

Looking at and creating a book nook alters one's perspective. Everything about it invites a shift in scale—suddenly, a tiny plant stem becomes a giant parasol tree; a plastic bottle cap transforms into a bucket, a lampshade, or even a well; a paper clip bends into a coat hanger; a flat thumbtack becomes a jar lid; and representing even the simplest objects (a dustpan, a hook, an envelope) becomes a real challenge—one that engages both ingenuity for the stimulated mind and dexterity for our ten giant fingers.

At little cost, everything becomes possible. It just takes an observant eye and patience. Book nooks offer me, as someone who comes from both a literary and artistic/crafting/DIY/interior design background, a new way to practice the philosophy that has guided all of my past projects: seeing gold in the ordinary. Having spent my childhood making gifts by hand, writing stories, and creating theatrical productions (including the set designs), book nooks synthesize all these forms of arts and crafts—creating a closed space to cultivate an imaginary, three-dimensional world.

Yet, after spending long hours and nights absorbed in creating these boxes (with some requiring over forty hours of meticulous work), I have realized that when it comes to illusion, the most disorienting factor is not the shift in perspective but rather the manipulation of time. Let me explain: Immersing oneself in the miniature blurs your sense of scale, but what you lose far more is your perception of time passing.

Take yourself somewhere outside the constraints of time and instead pour wax into tiny pieces of drinking straws to make candles just half an inch tall, or peg miniature paper laundry onto an ant-sized clothesline, or shine a pinpoint of light into an acorn-cap lampshade; these seemingly absurd acts bring a hint of bliss—a bubble of timelessness.

In this absorption, one touches the pure joy of creating something that exists solely for its own sake. Semiotician Tzvetan Todorov defined art in this way, using the word *autotelic*—finding its purpose within itself. Drawing from both my readings and hands-on experience, I like to believe that book nooks are more than just decoration. They embody a certain wisdom, offering a path to inner peace. As Lao Tzu once said: "The perception of the infinitely small is the secret of clairvoyance; the protection of the infinitely fragile and tender is the secret of strength."

This book invites you to pause time and use your hands to open a gap in the material world where dreams unfold. It offers over twenty themed ideas as creative starting points. Now it is up to you to carve out your own paths in the hidden spaces winding between the treasures of your bookshelf, guided by the light of your imagination.

BOXES

DIMENSIONS

This is the starting point for creating a miniature world: the frame that will fit between your books. First, choose the spot on your bookshelf where you want to display your book nook. The surprise effect will be more magical if it does not stick out too much from the other books. In terms of width, choose something between 3 and 9 inches (8 and 23 cm). In terms of height, it could be between the size of a small paperback and a large hardcover, anywhere from 4¼ to 12 inches (11 to 30 cm). The depth determines how immersive the scene can be, ideally between 4 and 10 inches (10 and 25 cm).

MATERIALS

A sturdy cardboard box is a great place to start. You can reinforce and enhance it by adding a decorative front frame (see pages 60, 66, 94, and 124). Consider covering the outside with textured wallpaper samples or scrapbook paper that looks like wood or stone.

For a more durable option, wood is an excellent choice: ¼-inch (5-mm) MDF board or plywood is inexpensive, easy to cut, and simple to decorate. Use small nails to hold the pieces together during assembly, then secure them permanently with wood glue.

ASSEMBLY

Assemble only the base, one sidewall, and the back panel first. This leaves you more space to arrange the interior. Attach the second wall at the end and save the top panel for last.

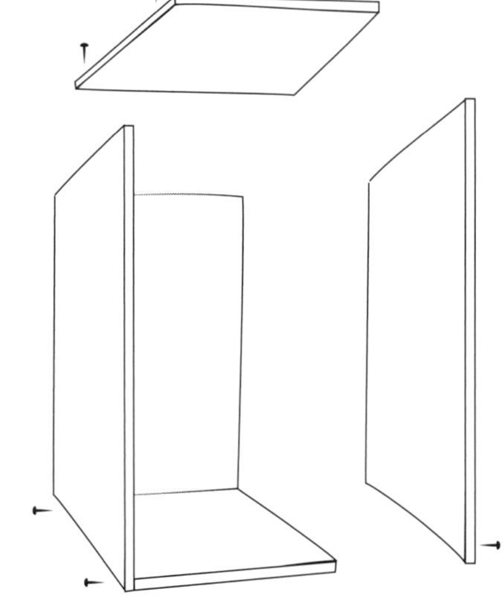

A simple cardboard box works perfectly, whether from recycled packaging or hand-made using thick honeycomb cardboard.

Keep an eye out in grocery stores for bulk or display boxes.

File boxes can also work. The top can even be cut to fill in the missing triangle of space.

A small polystyrene crate provides a sleek thickness and allows you to easily pin objects into it.

A wooden box is ideal. Premade options are available, like this bamboo planter.

Wooden or card-board tissue boxes have an existing opening that can inspire creative designs.

Secondhand metal boxes can be displayed vertically to the side and can be hollowed out or left partly open.

A set of books can be transformed into a hidden, built-in scene. See pages 38, 52, 80, and 158.

Two narrow drawers stacked together create nice depth—remove the bottom of one or create an open-worked divider.

Building a box from a picture frame is always an elegant choice (see pages 70, 80, and 100). Here, a key box was used.

A double-sided box with a central divider can be two book nooks in one! Simply flip it around to change the scene.

The same idea multiplied by four—for example, a four-season book nook that you can rotate.

TOOLS

You can start making book nooks without any special tools other than the basics: a sharp crafting knife, fine scissors (such as nail scissors), a cutting mat to protect your table, a sharp point tool for making holes (a nail or screw can work in a pinch), and tweezers.

PRECISION TWEEZERS

It is nevertheless worth investing in long precision tweezers (8–10 inches/20–25 cm long) or curved tweezers, which make it easier to reach deep into boxes. You can find them in philatelic (stamp collecting) shops or aquarium supply stores.

GLUE

Three types of glue are essential:

- White vinyl glue (wood glue), which is applied with a brush and dries clear
- Hot glue (but you must be very quick, and it leaves annoying strands)
- Precision glue, less known and pictured below, with a fine nozzle and pointed cap. This makes detailed work much easier.

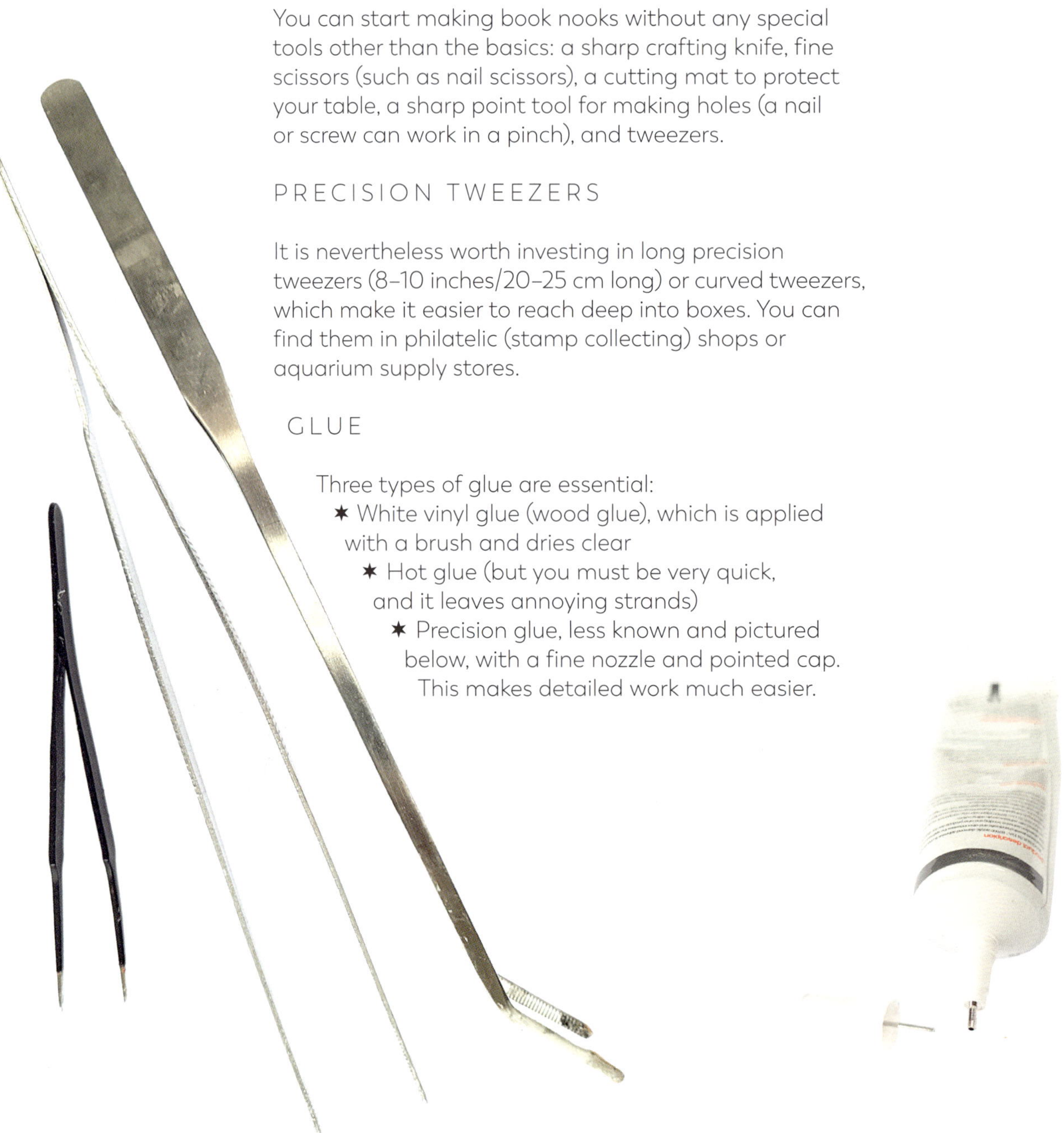

Among these basic tools for creating miniatures, the addition of three specialized tools can make a big difference.

PRECISION KNIFE PEN

The green tool in the photo looks like a pen, but instead of a tip, it has an ultrathin blade, so that you can even cut paper lace.

MICRON PEN

Incredibly fine tip! If you have sharp eyesight, you can write on the head of a pushpin.

HAND DRILL

The tool in the photo between the gimlet and the awl is a hand drill. It uses ultrafine bits and is turned by hand—perfect for making tiny holes!

LIGHTING

Adding lighting to the book nook is a crucial step. The lighting will enhance the magic of the little world lost among the books. It catches the eye, softens the outlines, highlights the details, and colors the atmosphere. One could even say that each scene has two looks: day and night.

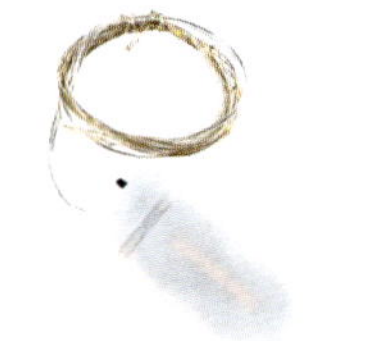

To keep it simple, all of the book nooks in this book were made using these three types of lighting options, on their own or a combination:

- A thin string of LED lights with button cell batteries
- A string of LED lights with stick-shaped ends, powered by AAA batteries
- An ultraflat coaster light with button cell batteries

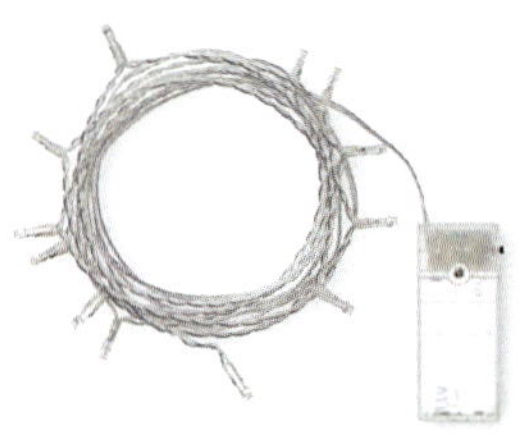

The first option is the most convenient. Very thin and flexible, it is discreet and can fit into all the corners of the display. It comes in different varieties:

- White light (strong and cool), warm light (yellow and cozy), a single color, or multicolored
- With a very flat casing (like the one in the top photo) or with a small but thick casing, the size of a sugar cube
- From 3 to 10 feet (1 to 3 meters) in length

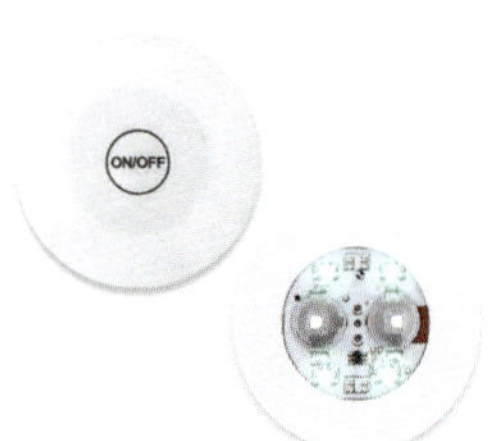

The second option is slightly bulkier but has a more powerful effect.

The 2½-inch (6-cm) diameter coaster light is very practical with its button switch when you want to illuminate a single point. It usually requires piercing a hole in the box.

CREATIVE IDEAS

You can also explore ultraviolet lights, mini flashlight key chains, battery-powered fiber-optic bouquets, light-up earrings, backpack lights, LED dog collar pendant lights, not to mention all the materials available for model making and dollhouses.

INDEX OF ITEMS

Ready to get started? During your creation process, you may find yourself wondering how to make this or that object. This list should help you find inspiration for repurposing everyday objects and materials.

EASY-TO-MAKE BOOK NOOKS

A forest house made of bark,
a wintry landscape in a miniature wardrobe,
a luminous sculpture made of mirror shards,
a flight of butterflies escaping from a book,
a charcoal cliff that glows in the dark,
a kitsch fawn in a surprising hiding place,
a mountainside cascade made of real rocks,
a tiny tent perched high on wire legs,
a fairy-tale scene made entirely of paper,
and the dreamy trick of the infinite mirror. . .

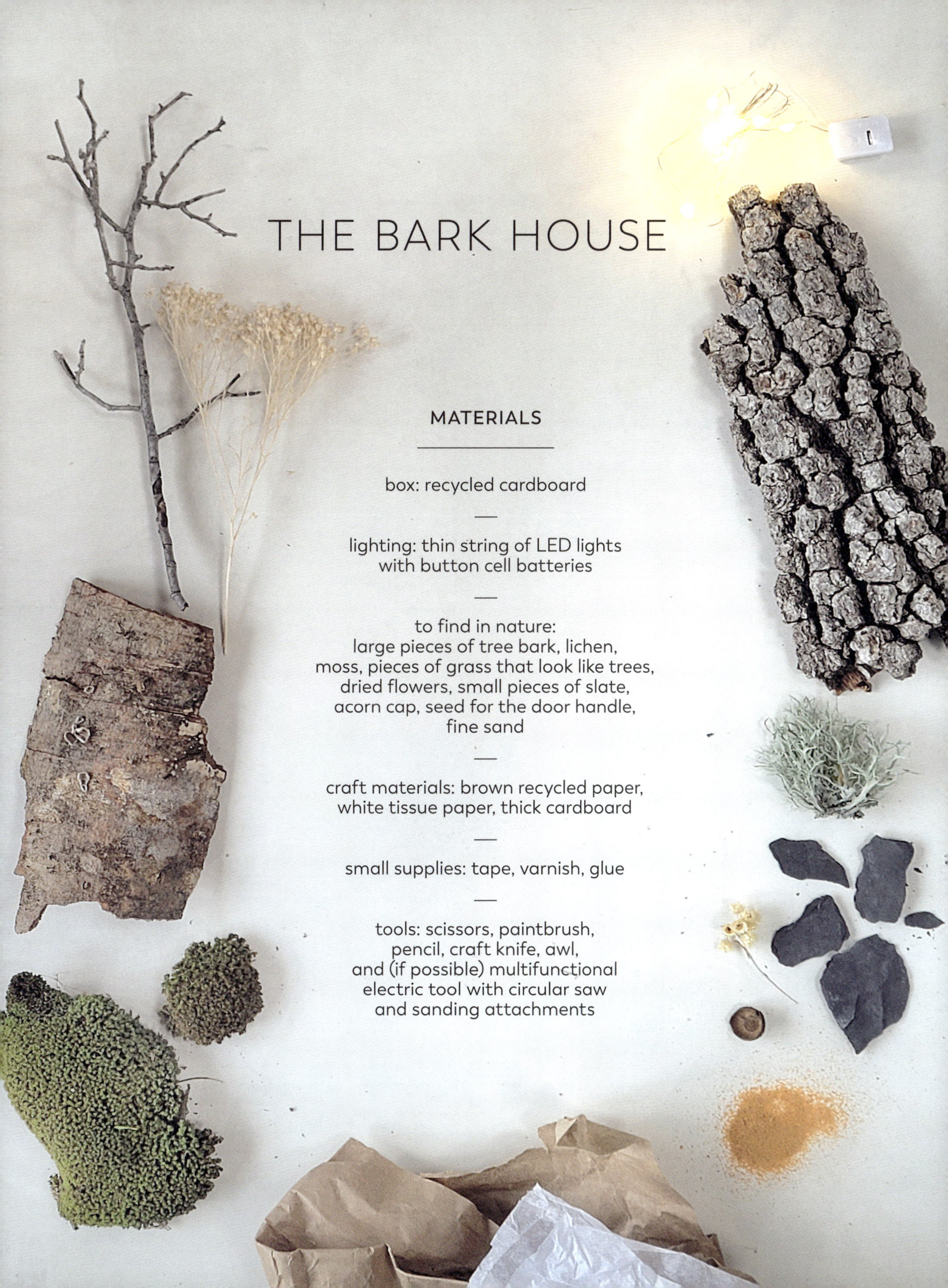

THE BARK HOUSE

MATERIALS

box: recycled cardboard

—

lighting: thin string of LED lights
with button cell batteries

—

to find in nature:
large pieces of tree bark, lichen,
moss, pieces of grass that look like trees,
dried flowers, small pieces of slate,
acorn cap, seed for the door handle,
fine sand

—

craft materials: brown recycled paper,
white tissue paper, thick cardboard

—

small supplies: tape, varnish, glue

—

tools: scissors, paintbrush,
pencil, craft knife, awl,
and (if possible) multifunctional
electric tool with circular saw
and sanding attachments

Covering the Back and Sides

A SMALL HOUSE THAT IS SIMPLE TO MAKE USING NATURAL AND RECYCLED MATERIALS.

1 | Cover a box with crumpled brown recycled paper to resemble the walls of a cave, leaving some parts unglued to add thickness. Choose a thin, curved piece of bark that will form the house and trim it to fit the box.

2 | Choose another contrasting piece of bark (dark and rough) for the back. Trim it to fit the box and glue it in place.

3 | Glue a third piece of bark to the ceiling.

4 | Cut out the window using the circular saw of a small rotary tool. Keep the piece that was removed.

5 | Cut two small pieces of tissue paper and fold them to form two curtains. Glue them to the back of the window.

The Details

6 | Use the same cutting tool to mark the contours of the door without fully cutting it out. Sand it gently and add varnish to make it a slightly different shade.

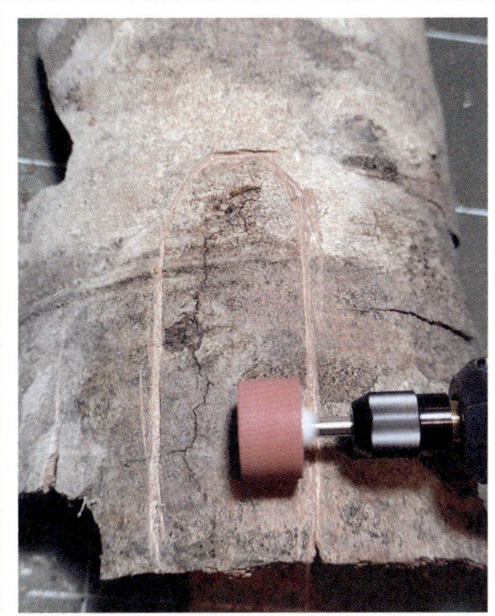

7 | Make the mailbox using the small piece of bark taken from the window, cut in half and glued next to the door.

8 | Create a small flap on the right side of the box to access the switch for the light string.

9 | Glue a small seed in place as the door handle. Use a gimlet (or a screw) to drill a hole next to the upper left side of the door. Cut the acorn cup with scissors and fit it on the facade to serve as a lampshade. Glue it in place. Place the battery pack for the string of lights at the entrance of the flap and run the wire inside the box. The second LED bulb from the battery pack should be in the right position to poke through the hole in the lampshade on the house's facade.

The Setup

10 | Make a small stand out of sturdy cardboard and glue it to the back of the bark house to keep it upright and stable.

11 | Stick two LED bulbs behind the curtains and glue the wire down. The wire should extend from the top of the house on the right side. Glue the base of the house to the box. Attach a sprig of grass to act as a tree on the right wall and wrap the string lights around it. Glue another piece of grass on the left side, along with the lichen and moss.

12 | Hide the remaining LED bulbs behind the dried flowers and plant materials. Break the slate into small tiles. Apply glue to the floor and add the tiles. Sprinkle the fine sand over them, then blow on the floor gently to remove the excess sand.

SEPT ETRANGERS
Pierre Chanlaine
Cocktail Sentimental
Editions
A LA BELLE HELENE
LUC RIVIÈRE
CH. VÉLAIN
COURS

THE WINTRY KINGDOM

MATERIALS

box: small dollhouse wardrobe and thin plywood

—

lighting: thin string of LED lights with button cell batteries

—

to gather: artificial snow spray, two black straws, two small black rubber washers (or rubber bands), sprigs of juniper or pine, fabric or washi tape with old-fashioned pattern

—

craft materials: small piece of cardboard, tracing paper or parchment paper, cotton batting

—

small materials: glitter, black bead, white and blue paint, white glue, white pencil, sandpaper, adhesive tape

—

tools: small saw, paintbrush, glue gun, craft knife, scissors, drill with a fine wood bit

Assembling the Box

Discover a winter landscape, inspired by the world of Narnia, hidden behind a dollhouse wardrobe.

1 | Take measurements of your miniature wardrobe and shelf and cut five pieces of thin plywood to form the sides, roof, base (aligned with the inside of the wardrobe), and back of the box. Sand the edges.

2 | Remove the back of the wardrobe; it will not be used.

3 | Glue the pieces of the box together, except for one of the sidewalls.

Creating the Background

4 | Separate the cotton into several layers and cut out mountain shapes. Glue them onto the back and the sidewall, with the fluffy side visible, playing with the layers.

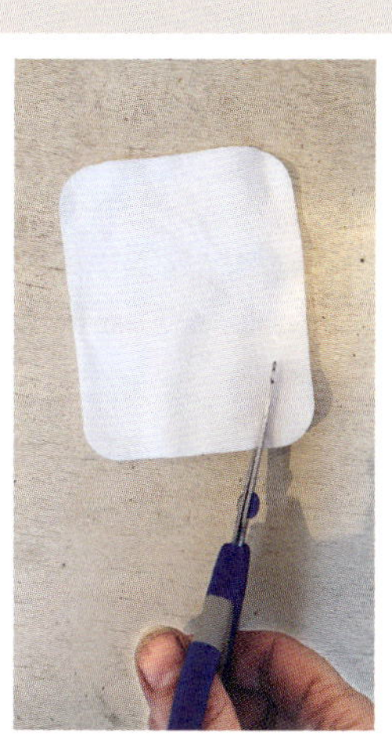

5 | Paint the sky blue with gouache paint, then dilute it with small touches of white before the first layer dries.

6 | Sprinkle glitter on the still-wet paint so that it sticks.

Making the Lamppost

7 | Reproduce the drawing of the lantern on a thin piece of cardboard or card stock (for example, a recycled cardboard envelope).

8 | Cut out the windows with a craft knife and hollow out the center of each part. Mark the folds along the dotted lines.

9 | Paint or color the outside black, and glue small pieces of tracing paper or parchment paper on the inside to mimic the glass panes.

10 | Cut the end of one straw into a star shape and poke it through the lantern, then glue the cut pieces to the inside.

11 | Bring together the four sides of the lantern by gluing the edges, then thread the end of the string of lights through the straw so that three LED bulbs stick out. Twist the wire to fill the available space inside the lantern.

12 | Take the second straw and cut off a section measuring 2½ inches (6 cm). Split it open and cut four long teeth, as if making a fork.

13 | Slide this section onto the base of the streetlamp along with two rubber washers. Push them up to create a wavy effect with the cut strips. Cut off any excess.

Assembly

14 | Drill holes in the base of the box in the places where you want to place the pine branches, the lamppost, and the rest of the string of lights. Opt for an asymmetrical arrangement. Remove the lamppost to complete the finishing touches: glue the top edges of the lamp with quick-dry glue and hold them closed until it sets. Add a black bead to the top.

15 | Spray the scene (without the lamppost) with snow spray.

16 | Spray the plain side of the other panel as well, creating a blurred horizon line.

Behind the Scenes

17 | Stick the lamp-post into the hole. Cut the base of the straw to form a star that will poke through underneath.

18 | Secure the base of the lamppost and the trees, as well as the electrical control box, with quality adhesive tape, ensuring that the switch remains accessible when the box is lifted.

19 | Run the string of lights along the inside edges of the box and glue it down with a hot glue gun, hiding the LED bulbs under small pieces of cotton.

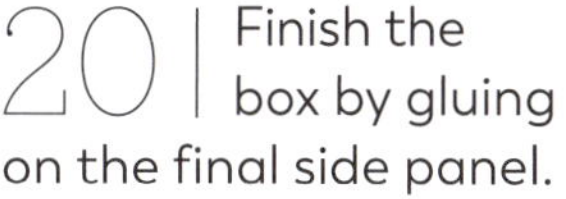

20 | Finish the box by gluing on the final side panel.

Final Touches

21 | Use a pencil to draw footprints in the snow.

22 | Cover the back of the wardrobe door with retro-patterned washi or fabric tape.

23 | Cover the other joints of the box with the same tape, then continue drawing the footprints on the wooden threshold with a white pencil.

POCKET
10
18
10
18
DELPHINE DE VIGAN
Paul Auster
GRÉGOIRE BOUILLIER

THE ICE PALACE

MATERIALS

box: sturdy recycled cardboard

—

lighting: battery-powered string of LED lights with rigid bulbs

—

relatively thick shards of broken mirror

—

imitation wood wallpaper or scrapbook paper

—

small materials: fabric or washi tape, spray glue

—

tools: hot glue gun, scissors, craft knife

Building the Cave

An ice cave made entirely from shards of a broken mirror. The little bears are optional.

1 | Choose a sturdy cardboard box and gather the large broken mirror shards. Be sure to protect yourself with gloves. If possible, work with the shards as they are, taking advantage of their random shapes, rather than attempting to cut them.

2 | Place some large pieces on the bottom to form a slope leading upward, then a sidewall and a sort of terrace supported (on the right) by this wall: this arrangement adds volume and creates a stage. Stick these fragments together using a hot glue gun, being sure to glue the pieces to each other, but not to the box.

3 | Next, glue some of the more elongated and pointed fragments to form a vaulted ceiling. Finish assembling the cave by gluing the small pieces. The sculpture should be stable and cohesive; it should not stick to the cardboard. Gently remove it from the box. Check its stability and sturdiness. If needed, reinforce it by adding more glue or even more additional support pieces.

Lighting

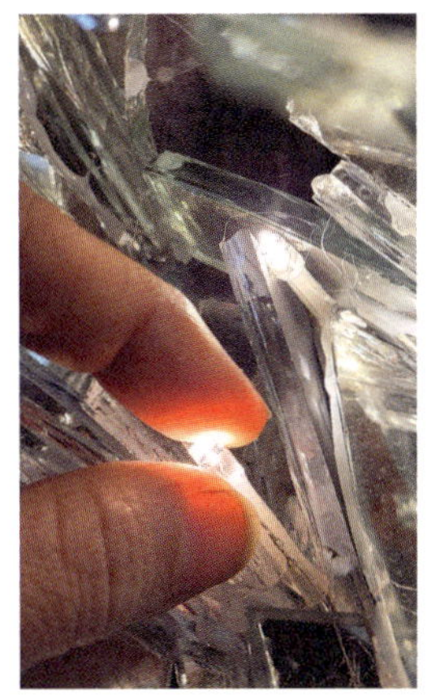

4 | Glue the string of lights to the back of the sculpture, positioning the LED bulbs in strategic spots so that they will light up the mirrors without causing a glare. Make the battery case accessible through a side hatch.

5 | Cover the outside of the box with imitation wood wallpaper or scrapbook paper and place the sculpture inside.

THE FLIGHT OF BUTTERFLIES

MATERIALS

thick hardcover book (to sacrifice)

—

lighting: thin string of LED lights
with button cell batteries in a flat case

—

small materials: butterfly-shaped decorative punch,
glue, duct tape

—

optional: additional butterflies made of paper
or translucent material

—

tools: small scissors, craft knife, hot glue gun

Transforming the Book

NOT REALLY A BOOK NOOK, BUT A BOOK TRANSFORMED INTO A SURPRISE. PLACE IN THE OPPOSITE DIRECTION OF THE OTHERS TO MAKE IT LOOK AS IF THE WORDS ARE FLYING OFF THE PAGES.

1 | Use a craft knife to make four evenly spaced ¾-inch (2-cm) slits at the top of the book's pages.

2 | Fold a piece of duct tape around the light string's battery case, with the sticky side facing out, and slide it into the spine to create a small pocket stuck to the inside that will prevent the case from falling to the bottom.

3 | Thread the string of lights through the four slits in multiple loops to spread the lights between the pages. Secure the string with dots of glue.

Cutting Out the Butterflies

4 | Use the decorative punch to cut out butterflies from the written or illustrated pages of the book.

5 | Draw additional butterflies by hand and cut them out with scissors.

6 | Since you need to make many of them, you can speed things up by folding the paper in half and cutting both sides of the butterfly together.

Gluing the Butterflies

7 | Glue the butterflies onto both the edges of the pages, after slightly folding their wings, as well as onto the wires of the string of lights. You can also add printed pictures of butterflies. Mix different sizes and colors while maintaining a cohesive color palette. Finish by gluing together the pages, hiding the loops of the light string.

THE PHOSPHORESCENT CLIFF

MATERIALS

box: premade bamboo

—

lighting: battery-powered string of lights with eight LED black light sticks

—

to buy: small glow-in-the-dark figurines (can also be made with fluorescent modeling clay)

—

to find in nature: charcoal pieces, burned wood planks, moss, twigs with lichen

—

small materials: small rubber band, white glue

—

tools: small handsaw, hot glue gun, paintbrush, precision tweezers

Creating the Backdrop

EASY TO CREATE THANKS TO THE NATURAL SCULPTURES OFFERED BY CHARCOAL, THIS WORLD EVOKES THE FILMS OF HAYAO MIYAZAKI AND TRULY COMES TO LIFE WITH THE BLACK LIGHTS. WHEN THE BOX IS TURNED OFF, THE LITTLE SPIRITS GLOW.

1 | Gather pieces of burned wood taken from a stove or fireplace. Pay particular attention to the appearance of the wood plank that will serve as the background. A small crack at the top is a nice touch.

2 | Saw out a rectangle on the bottom right of the background plank to create a space that will allow access to the battery case (located at the bottom right of the composition).

Adding the Lighting

3 | Secure the LED bulbs together in a bundle with a rubber band except for the two closest to the battery pack, which should be left free.

4 | Glue the string of lights to the back of the plank, making sure to leave the two free LED bulbs sticking out above, at the level of the top crack.

5 | Position the main plank inside the box, edge to edge, tilted slightly back, with the LED bundle in the center and the battery pack sliding into the designated opening. Use a hot glue gun to secure the plank in place, as well as the LED bundle, after spreading out its base to ensure stability.

The Composition

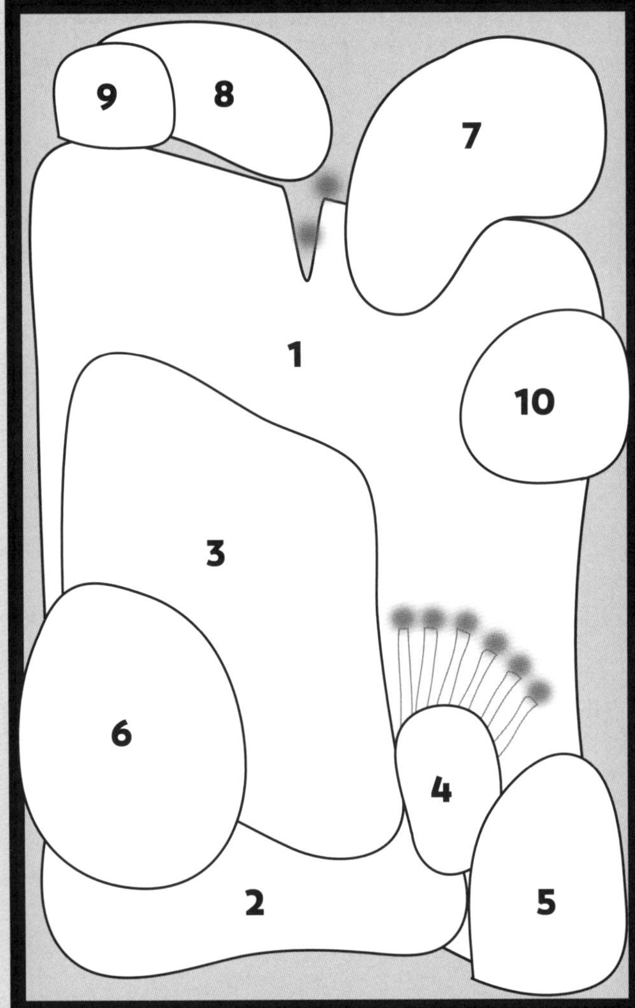

6 | Just as in Zen gardens, the arrangement of the blocks may appear random and natural, but it is actually a carefully planned composition designed to create harmony within asymmetry. Take the time to experiment with different placements using the charcoal blocks available to you.

The suggested layout for this composition is as follows:
1: The main plank serving as the cliff in the background, tilted slightly back.
2: A base on which the small crowd of luminous beings will be placed.
3: A smaller cliff, almost parallel to the first, creating a dark gap between them from which the bundled lights will emerge. This cliff will be adorned with vegetation along its visible edge.
4: A small background block that conceals the base of the lamp.
5: A removable block that hides the battery case.
6: A foreground rock on the left that will support a tree.
7, 8, 9: Rocks placed on the cliff.
10: Save this spot for the most interesting block, which will be suspended in place with glue.
Additional fragments can be added afterward to unify the composition.

Securing the Base

7 | Glue moss onto the most visible edge of block 3. Work carefully, starting with a layer of short moss, then adding a few more distinct strands on top.

8 | Glue the base (2) with a hot glue gun, followed by the small mossy cliff (3). Conceal the bottom of the light string by gluing block 4. If needed, add a few charcoal fragments in order to fill in gaps and create a relatively level scene.

9 | Use a brush to cover the entire surface of the small charcoal rock (5) with white glue, as it will be used to hide the battery pack. Let it dry on a nonstick surface. This is the only piece that will not be fixed in place—the white glue (which dries clear) is meant to prevent crumbling, so that it will not leave black dust on fingers when handled.

Completing the Landscape

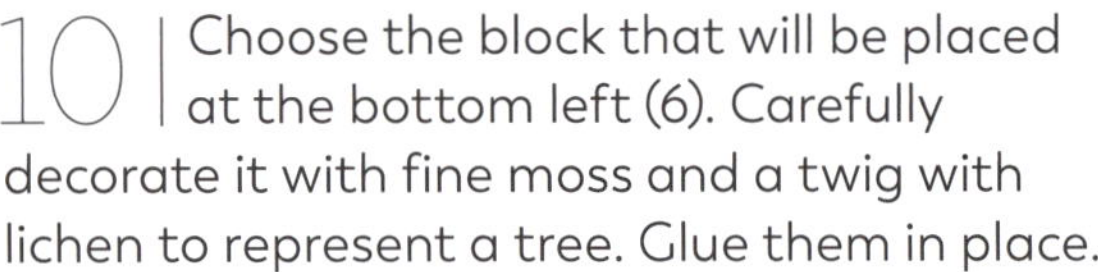

10 | Choose the block that will be placed at the bottom left (6). Carefully decorate it with fine moss and a twig with lichen to represent a tree. Glue them in place.

11 | Next, select blocks 7, 8, and 9, which will be positioned at the very top of the main plank, leaving small horizontal spaces where some luminous beings can be placed. Glue these in place using a hot glue gun.

Arranging the Little Creatures

12 | Place the little creatures wherever you like and glue them in place using a hot glue gun. A precision tool, such as retractable claw tweezers (shown in the photo), can be helpful for handling and positioning them. Some can be glued directly onto the LED bulbs if desired.

13 | Glue the last rock (10) along with another tree adorned with lichen, then add small pieces of rock to hide the joints, as well as little trumpet-shaped pieces of lichen in the foreground.

THE MAGIC CAVERN

MATERIALS

large hardcover book (to sacrifice)

—

lighting: thin string of multicolored LED lights with button cell batteries

—

to gather: small piece of glass (from a small frame), miniature fawn figurine, small mushroom

—

small materials: glitter, rhinestones, adhesive tape, blue masking tape, saucier spoon (or a straw), glue

—

tools: drill with a 1-inch (about 26-mm) spade drill bit, clamps, jigsaw, craft knife, ruler, precision tweezers, paintbrush

Creating the Cavern

THIS BOOK NOOK DOES NOT FIT BETWEEN TWO VOLUMES, BUT RATHER IN THE HEART OF ONE OF THEM. IN A DISCARDED OLD BOOK, A TINY MYSTERIOUS WORLD IN A CAVERN IS HIDDEN BEHIND GLASS.

1 | Keep the large book closed using clamps with spacers and drill into the spine to a depth of about 1¼ inch (3 cm) using a 1-inch (about 26-mm) spade drill bit.

2 | Expand the hole with a jigsaw, then cut a rectangle the size of the piece of glass out of the spine with a craft knife. Tear the edges of the pages inside the hole to create irregular walls.

3 | Open the book to glue the string lights in place with the wires hidden and the LED bulbs sticking out, spread out along the walls. Leave bits of words sticking out.

Adding the Fairy Dust

4 | Glue green glitter on the floor of the cave, then add the rhinestones, the fawn, and the mushroom (toy or handmade). Form stalactites using a hot glue gun. Cover the frame to the cave with silver glitter. Glue on the glass rectangle and finish with blue masking tape around the edge.

5 | It may help to use a saucier spoon from the kitchen accessories section, or you can make a DIY version by permanently pinching a small spoon. Another solution is to cut a straw at an angle.

THE MOUNTAIN CASCADE

MATERIALS

box: an old metal cookie tin

—

lighting: ultraflat LED coaster light powered by button cell batteries

—

from nature: irregular stone covered in moss, flat stones, small pebbles, gravel, dried umbelliferous plant

—

to gather:
small round mirror for the moon,
miniature model figurines,
fiber fill stuffing (or cotton balls),
small piece of foam board
(or other thick cardboard),
wide wooden craft sticks

—

small materials: glue, paint

—

tools: hot glue gun, scissors, craft knife, paintbrush, precision tweezers

The Background

PARTICULARLY EASY TO CREATE, THIS LANDSCAPE RELIES ON THE CHOICE OF THE MAIN STONE, WHICH INVITES US TO CHANGE THE SCALE OF OUR PERSPECTIVE.

2 | To light it very simply, create a small ceiling support made of two wide craft sticks, with the ends farthest into the box glued to two layers of foam board. In the space thus created, a removable coaster light can be inserted, which can be slid forward with a finger to extract and turn on or off.

1 | Try several positions for the main stone, then choose three pointed flat stones as a background. Glue, in order, a piece of fiber fill or cotton stuffing as a cloud, then a small round mirror (or a disc cut from silver paper) to make the moon, another cloud, the largest of the pointed stones, then another on top (it was broken to obtain the white edges standing out). Glue the other peak next to it. Then, place the large main rock in the foreground to form the mountain.

The Cascade

3 | Pour hot glue with a glue gun, pulling on the still-warm flow to form strands that will solidify instantly (easy to achieve).

4 | Paint the strands blue and green, along with the pond. Cover the edge of the pond with white glue and stick gravel and small pebbles onto it. Finally, glue down the umbelliferous plant and the small white figurines.

THE TENTS IN THE CLOUDS

MATERIALS

box: recycled cardboard and frame
from a small wooden crate

—

lighting: thin string of LED lights
with button cell batteries

—

craft materials: crate or craft wood, white tissue paper,
wallpaper or scrapbook paper to cover the box,
white air-dry clay

—

to gather: various dried plants and grasses,
fine white gravel

—

small materials: wire, string, glue, adhesive tape,
cotton batting, artificial snow spray (optional)

—

tools: craft knife, wire cutter,
precision tweezers, scissors, paintbrush

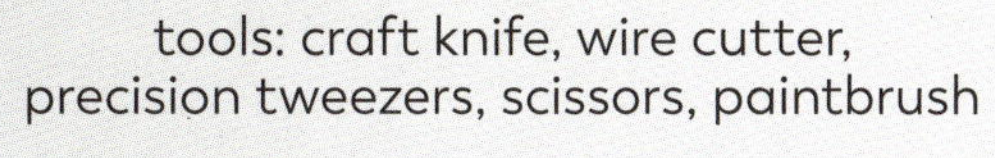

The Tents

BORN FROM A DESIRE FOR LIGHTNESS TUCKED BETWEEN HEAVY BOOKS, LITTLE HOUSES ARE PERCHED ON LONG WIRE LEGS IN AN IMAGINARY LANDSCAPE.

1 | Twist two long strands of wire together at the middle.

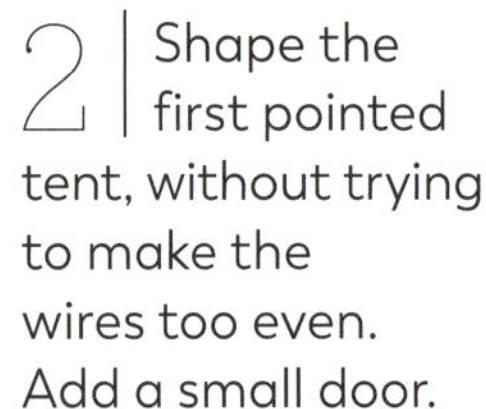

2 | Shape the first pointed tent, without trying to make the wires too even. Add a small door.

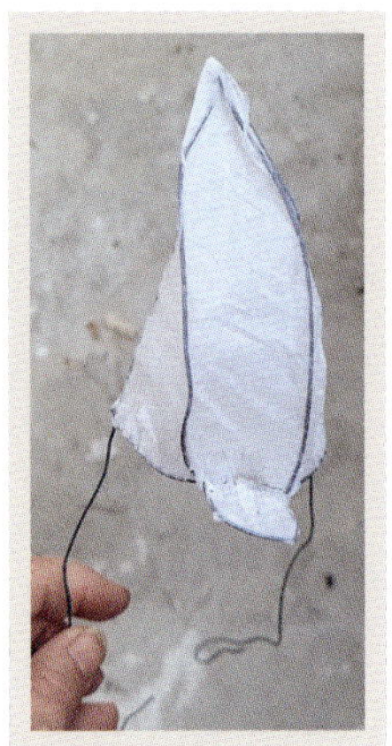

3 | Create a second, slightly different tent, which will be placed against the left wall in the foreground.

4 | Cover the tents with pieces of tissue paper using a paintbrush coated with white glue.

The Frame and the Details

5 | Roll small balls of air-dry clay by hand, insert a small piece of dried plant into each, press to flatten each base, and let dry.

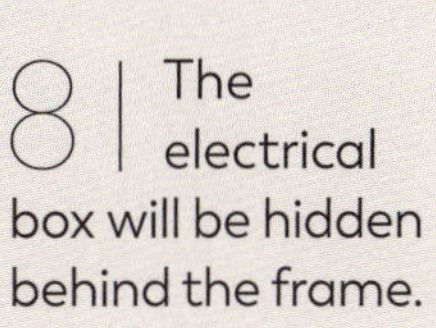

8 | The electrical box will be hidden behind the frame.

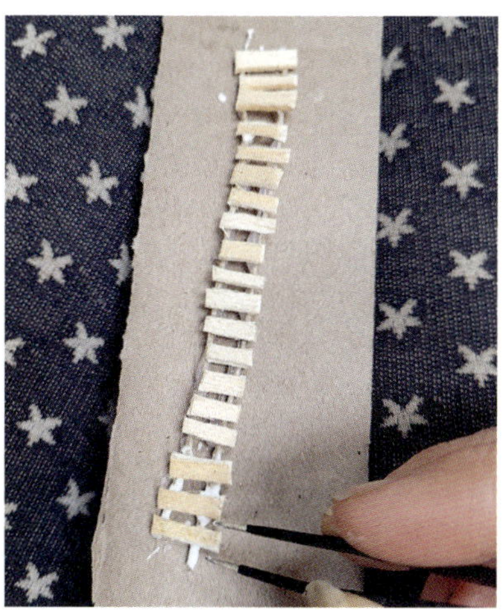

6 | Cut strips of crate or craft wood and glue them onto two parallel strings to make the ladder. Attach it to the door of the first tent.

7 | Cover the outside of the box with wallpaper or scrapbook paper and glue together a frame made of crate wood pieces.

Finishing Touches

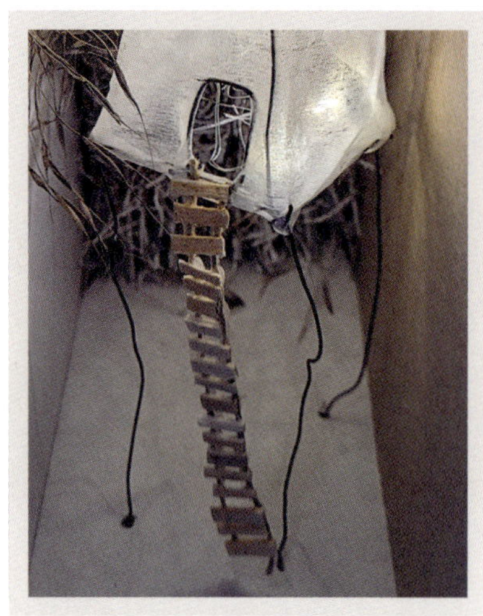

9 | Use wire to secure a bundle of dried grass to a piece of cardboard the size of the back of the box. Spray artificial snow at the bottom (optional as this is not very noticeable; white spray paint can also be used or this step can be omitted).

10 | Attach the electrical box behind the frame at the top left. Run the wire along the ceiling and through the grasses. Secure the tent legs by passing them through the floor, taping them underneath, then thread the string light inside the back tent, behind the ladder, and finally into the foreground tent.

11 | Cover the floor with glue, then sprinkle fine white gravel over it. Dip the clay base of each little dried plant in glue and distribute the plants all over the floor. Finish by gluing clouds of cotton batting on the walls.

VICTOR HUGO
NOTRE-DAME DE PARIS
SELECTION DU LIVRE
CONGO
Alexandre Soljénitsyne

THE PAPER LANDSCAPE

MATERIALS

box: thick honeycomb cardboard

—

lighting: ultraflat LED coaster light
with button cell batteries

—

craft materials: white Canson paper
or other high-quality art paper, flat wooden sticks
(to make the frame)

—

small materials: adhesive tape, pencil, eraser

—

tools: precision craft knife, cutting mat, scissors,
ruler, hot glue gun, saw and miter box

Drawing and Cutting

WITH MINIMAL MATERIALS, LET THE BOLDNESS OF CUTTING WITH A CRAFT KNIFE AND THE MAGIC OF LIGHT PASSING THROUGH THE PAPER DO THE REST. I COLLABORATED WITH DESIGNER PAULINE COTTEREAU FOR THE PATTERNS.

1 | Cut five sheets of Canson or other high-quality art paper to your desired size. Enlarge these five patterns with a photocopier and trace them onto the paper. Alternatively, you can create your own designs. If that is the case, sketch the first layer for the foreground with a large central opening. Cut out its outline and open spaces. Place it on the second sheet as a guide and draw the next layer, continuing in the same way while ensuring certain details stand out through the openings, such as the owl in the tree here.

Assembly

2 | Cut the sides of the box. Use the tip of a pencil to score even grooves along the ridges of the honeycomb cardboard.

3 | Glue the base and one of the sides together, then slide each paper layer into the grooves.

4 | Assemble all four sides in this manner. Secure the edges with adhesive tape.

5 | Use a saw with a miter box to cut the sticks for the frame at 45-degree angles. Glue the frame onto the front edge of the cardboard box.

6 | Cut a hole in the back of the box where the coaster light will be placed. Glue the coaster light in place.

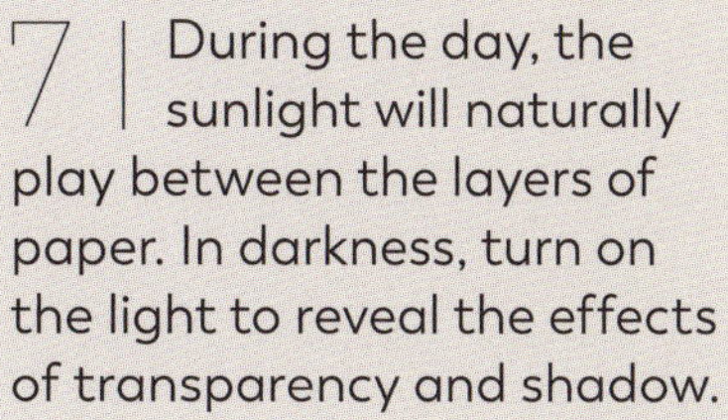

7 | During the day, the sunlight will naturally play between the layers of paper. In darkness, turn on the light to reveal the effects of transparency and shadow.

Editions de La Martinière
Masuji Ibuse Pluie noire
INOUE
Nuages garance
folio
BABEL
YOKO OGAWA • AMOURS EN MARGE
BABEL
YOKO OGAWA • LE MUSÉE DU SILENCE
YASUSHI
INOUÉ
La tuile de Tenpyô

THE INFINITE MIRROR

MATERIALS

box: sturdy recycled cardboard box

—

lighting: thin, battery-powered string of LED lights with gold foliage

—

essentials: frame with glass, mirror of the same size, roll of one-way mirror film for windows

—

small materials: fiber fill stuffing or fake snow (cotton balls can also work), white wire, wooden stir sticks, twig with lichen, white paint, vinyl glue

—

tools: hot glue gun, craft knife, scissors, paintbrush

The Setup

CREATE THE ILLUSION OF INFINITY BY PLACING A LIGHT BETWEEN A MIRROR AND A SHEET OF ONE-WAY MIRROR FILM.

1 | Build or modify a sturdy cardboard box the size of the mirror. Paint it white.

2 | Cut a piece of one-way mirror film to the size of the frame's glass. Moisten one side, apply it to the glass, and smooth out any bubbles.

3 | Glue the glass into the frame and cover the back with stuffing, fake snow, or cotton balls (pulled apart) to hide the edges.

4 | Line the inner edges of the box with the same cloudlike material.

5 | Make a hole in one side of the box, arrange the lights around the edges, attach the battery pack to the back.

6 | Wrap a piece of wire horizontally around the twig, which will appear repeatedly in the reflections.

Arranging the Infinite Scene

8 | Cut wooden stir sticks into curved segments and glue them together to form tracks. Add a small wire support and glue it firmly in a horizontal position.

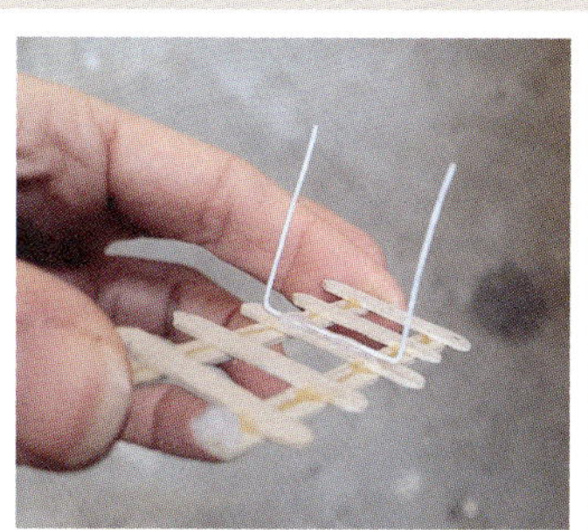

7 | Glue the tree in place. The ends of the wire should touch both mirrors.

9 | Glue on the frame to close the box, letting a few leaves stick out. Attach a piece of track on the outside, lined up with the track on the inside. When the lights are off, the interior is invisible. But once turned on, the magic happens: the scene reflects to infinity.

MORE AMBITIOUS PROJECTS

A monastery perched atop a log cliff,
an antiques shop filled with wonders
hidden between the pages,
a bakery inspired by traditional
Provençal nativity scenes,
a spiraling masterpiece of doodles,
an artist's studio straight out of Montmartre,
a colorful alleyway glowing under a streetlamp,
a tree house with roots dipping into the water,
a cozy library with a fireplace nook,
a retro kitchen bursting with color and detail,
a dreamlike sleeper train car with vintage charm,
an underground cave with a mysterious green lake,
and a Mexican hacienda created with a Chinese fan.

THE GREEK MONASTERY

MATERIALS

box: custom cut ¼-inch (5-mm) MDF or plywood

—

lighting: thin string of LED lights and ultraflat LED coaster light, both with button cell batteries

—

to salvage: old piece of soft wood, pieces of bark

—

craft materials: textured paper for the background, crate wood or craft wood, white air-dry clay

—

small supplies: white paint, gold leaf flakes, walnut stain (or diluted brown paint), matches, wire, twine, fabric tape, large nail

—

tools: saw, chisel, craft knife, pocketknife, gimlet, hand drill, drill bit with wings, pliers, scissors, paintbrush, hot glue gun

The Caves and Other Surprises

INSPIRED BY THE GEOLOGICAL WONDER OF METEORA, A LOG IS TRANSFORMED INTO A MYSTICAL JOURNEY.

1 | Choose a lightweight, weathered, crumbly piece of wood from the garden or forest that will be easy to carve. Saw it to fit inside the box and stand upright. Mark out a high platform for the monastery. Carve stairs and enlarge holes to make interconnected caves.

2 | To create protruding platforms, insert two small pieces of wire into the soft wood and place a piece of crate wood that has been cut with scissors and stained on top. A small strip of fabric tape can be added to mimic a railing.

3 | Add stairs and ladders made of wood and metal. Brush a little moistened clay onto the cave floors to enhance their appearance. You can line one of the caves with gold leaf.

Finishing Touches

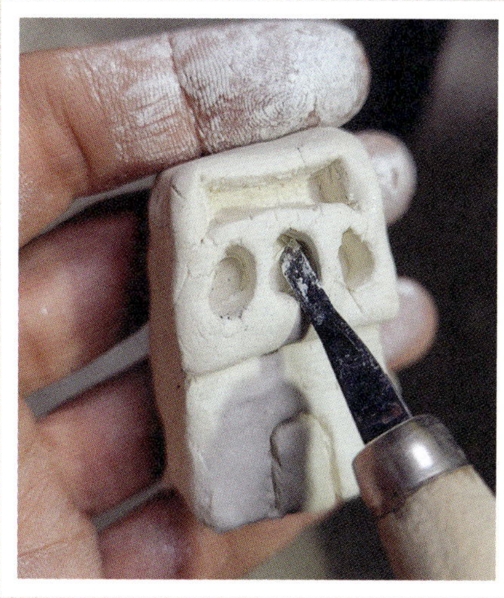

4 | Sculpt the monastery from white air-dry clay. If you make it hollow, the string of lights can pass through it, illuminating the windows.

5 | Shape the building onto the wood, add a roof, then lightly paint or stain it and glue a staircase to the facade.

6 | Choose a semirigid decorative paper to curve behind the log inside the box.

7 | Drill through the log and secure it onto a large upright nail at the base—this allows it to pivot, providing access to the hidden battery pack.

8 | Drill through the log to thread the string lights, ensuring they illuminate the caves, stairs, and buildings while keeping the wires as hidden as possible (this requires patience and precision). Glue the battery pack on the back. A ceiling light can be added using an LED coaster light, after drilling through the top of the box with a winged drill bit.

SÉLECTION DU LIVRE
SÉLECTION DU LIVRE
SÉLECTION DU LIVRE
SÉLECTION DU LIVRE
SÉLECTION DU LIVRE
SÉLECTION DU LIVRE
BROCANTE
CHRISTIAAN BARNARD UNE VIE
LE DIEU AUX YEUX VERTS

THE SECRET ANTIQUES SHOP

MATERIALS

structure: 7 large vintage books of the same size (to sacrifice), gold frame with glass

lighting: thin string of LED lights with button cell batteries

accessories to gather: small sculptures and other miniature trinkets, dollhouse dishes, pendants, earrings, medals, tiny figurines, mini bottles, stones, shells, beads

to repurpose: bell, hairpin, mini frames sold as nail decorations

small materials: thin flexible wire, glue, gold paper (chocolate wrapper)

tools: jigsaw, scissors, craft knife, ruler, precision pliers, hot glue gun

The Hollowed-out Books

A SURPRISE ON THE BOOKSHELF: HIDDEN INSIDE SOME OLD VOLUMES FOUND AT THE ANTIQUES SHOP IS . . . AN ANTIQUES SHOP. THIS PROJECT IS LESS ABOUT MAKING THAN GATHERING A WHOLE BUNCH OF MINIATURE TRINKETS.

1 | Position the frame on the edges of the group of books and mark the contours. Try to choose a frame that occupies the exact width of five spines. You will use the jigsaw to cut the books. The simplest method is to form a curve, then remove the rounded angle with two saw cuts.

2 | Cut three books in this way (they will be in positions 4, 5, and 6 in the final assembly). The height of the hole is the short side of the frame. The depth is the desired size of the store. Cut book #2 less deeply: it will represent the shop entrance. Book #3 is first cut the same way as #2, then the cover and pages are cut with the craft knife to form a sort of stairway for shelves. The last book is hollowed with the craft knife to create an alcove in its back cover. It will close the space on the right side.

The Display Shelves

3 | Cut the bookmark ribbon from one of the books (or, if none is available, use a thin ribbon). For a tailor's hack, hold the ribbon over boiling water so that the steam smooths it out. Glue it around the alcove of book #7 to form a frame. You can even make a shelf from the cover board scraps.

4 | Cut a section of the leftover scraps from book #2 (the hollow form in the photo comes from a hole made by a drill), open it in a fan shape, and cover it with a shelf. This will be the corner counter, which can be filled with objects.

5 | Make two small benches from cover scraps glued together. One will serve as a support at the back (in the photo, it is under the guitar), and the other as a display stand. Glue the miniature items to be sold onto them.

6 | Modify book #3 by gluing pages to the back to unify the cut pages and adding horizontal shelves from the leftover cover board. Fill it with small, glued-down objects, including mini books made from the scraps.

Lighting

7 | Cut a space in the back of book #7 where the light string's power pack will be hidden.

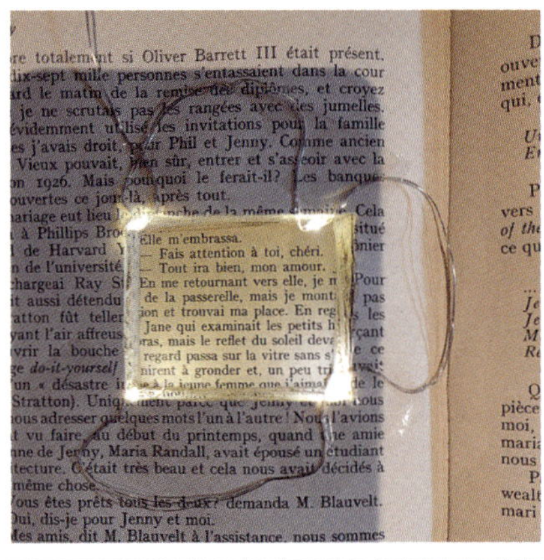

8 | Insert the light string into the pages of book #7 and glue it so that 4 LED bulbs illuminate the alcove. Then drill a hole into the book, including the back cover, so that the end of the light string appears at the top right of the alcove. You can run it along the ceiling to the display case at the top right corner.

9 | Glue the objects inside the alcove, then glue all the volumes together. Clamp or press them together with heavy items to dry.

10 | Twist the wires to reduce the space between each pair of LED bulbs by half. Insert each twist between the top pages, following the wiring diagram pictured.

Finishing Touches

11 | To make the sign, cover a piece of cardboard with gold paper from a chocolate wrapper, write the shop name, drill holes into it, thread it with some wire, attach it to a bent hairpin, and slide it into the spine of book #7. For the bell, tie a bell to the bookmark of book #1 (or an added ribbon).

12 | Finalize the arrangement. For example, on the walls, hang medals and mini gold frames sold as nail decor. In a jar, place a worm. At the entrance, hang a key chain with mini keys. For decoration, use colored metal confetti sold as table confetti. On the floor, add vases made of beads and tiny figurines. Once everything is ready, glue on the frame with its glass.

THE VILLAGE BAKERY

MATERIALS

box: made from scraps of engineered wood flooring

—

lighting: thin string of LED lights
powered by AAA batteries

—

craft materials: thin wood from a cigar box,
balsa wood strips, wooden crate,
cardboard, foam board, tracing paper,
parchment paper, natural clay,
air-dry or polymer clay, fabric scraps

—

to repurpose: chopsticks, skewers, craft sticks,
twigs, matches, cork, egg cartons, peanut shells,
dried plants, moss, sand, small stone

—

small supplies: wire, twine, nails,
clothespins, beads, glitter, paint, chalk, nail polish,
various kinds of glue (wood glue, hot glue,
white glue, and wallpaper glue)

—

tools: saw, craft knife,
ruler, hot glue gun, spatula,
paintbrush, blender,
precision tweezers

The Frame

To make better use of the vertical space in the book nook, it has been divided into two sections: a facade on the upper level and a deep space on the ground floor, designed in the style of traditional Provençal nativity scenes.

1 | Construct a box from leftover floorboards, approximately 7½ x 12 x 7½ inches (19 x 30 x 19 cm), with an upper level 5½ inches (14 cm) from the top, recessed by 2 inches (5 cm).

2 | Soften some clay with water and spread it over the floor.

3 | Draw tiles using a tool with a rounded point and let dry. Paint the tiles a bluish-gray shade, being careful not to fill the cracks. Sprinkle a bit of fine sand over the top.

4 | Trace a window on the back of a cigar box (or on balsa wood) using a large roll of tape for the curve. Cut it out with a craft knife and glue on a small piece of wood to serve as a window ledge.

5 | Moisten a strip of cardboard and shape it into a rounded lintel by pressing it over the same tape roll.

6 | Make the balcony from wire and doubled wooden strips above and below. Spray paint it black.

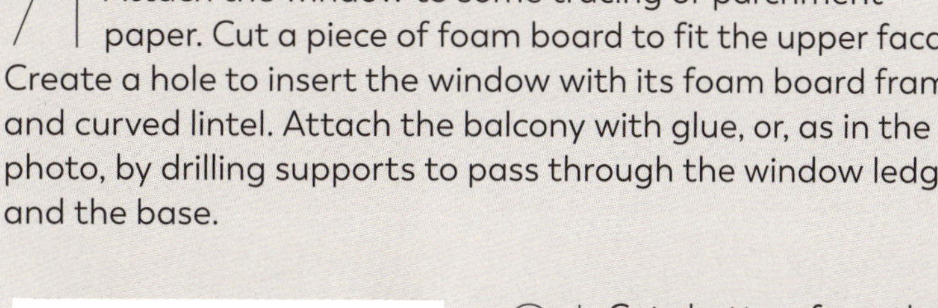

7 | Attach the window to some tracing or parchment paper. Cut a piece of foam board to fit the upper facade. Create a hole to insert the window with its foam board frame and curved lintel. Attach the balcony with glue, or, as in the photo, by drilling supports to pass through the window ledge and the base.

8 | Draw on the facade with pencil and chalk. Position it to be slightly set back from the frame. Fit a small roof of crate wood above the store and paint it.

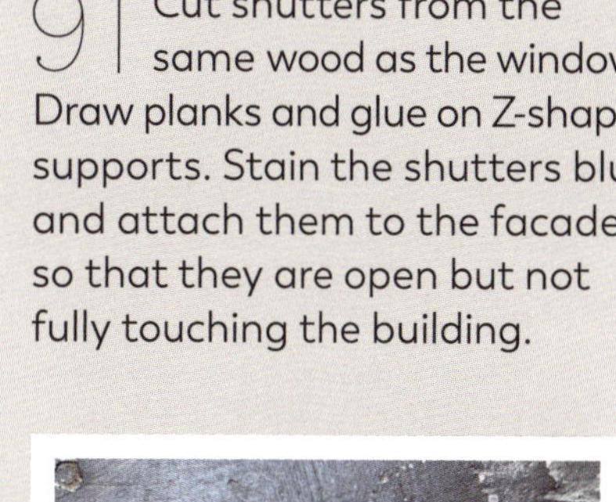

9 | Cut shutters from the same wood as the window. Draw planks and glue on Z-shaped supports. Stain the shutters blue and attach them to the facade so that they are open but not fully touching the building.

10 | Tear up an egg carton, soak the pieces in a bowl of water to soften them, and glue them onto the left wall of the ground floor and both sides of the frame.

11 | Save a bit of the egg carton for the chimney. Mix together the rest in a blender with enough water to create a pulp. Squeeze out any excess liquid if it seems too watery, then mix with flakes of wallpaper or textured paper. Create a foam board staircase 1½ inches (4 cm) deep to be placed at the back of the bakery. Cover it with the paper pulp and let dry.

The Bakery

12 | Shape the oven in relief using cardboard. Cover it with pieces of egg carton like the walls, then paint it white.

13 | For the oven door, glue small pieces of wood onto a rounded cut piece of cardboard. Smooth the edges with white air-dry clay.

14 | Make a shelf out of cardboard to attach to the right wall. Cover with clay, then paint and glue to the wall.

15 | Tie four small bunches of dried plants to a twig with wire, then affix it to the left wall. Glue the staircase in the back of the scene and the oven at an angle in front.

16 | To make the counter, cut four wooden chopsticks for legs and attach two craft stick frames.

17 | Midway up the counter, a balsa wood tray with notched corners rests on small matchstick supports.

18 | Against the left wall, glue two cork slices under a small piece of wood to display pastries.

19 | To make the lampshade, coat a small stone with oil and wrap it in oiled parchment paper. Soak 3 yards of kitchen twine in white glue and wrap it around the stone. Let it dry, then cut it into a shell shape and remove the paper.

The Miniature Food

201

Create various types of bread, cakes, and pastries using white air-dry clay. Paint them and arrange them throughout the bakery. For colored glazes, use nail polish and glitter as sugar.

Finishing Touches

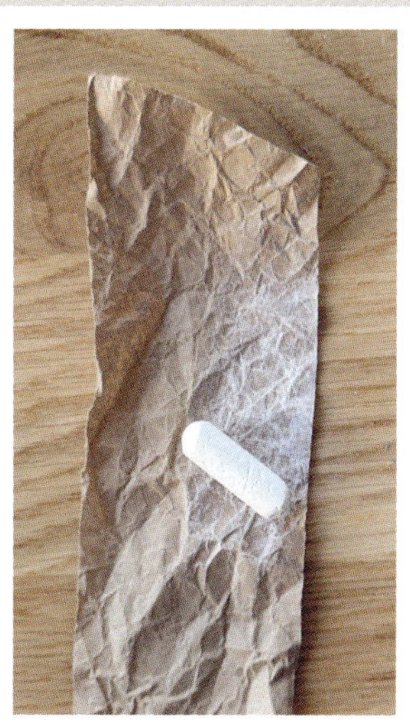

21 | Distribute the pastries among the various displays. Attach the shelf to the right wall. To cover the front of the right wall, rub chalk onto crumpled kraft paper and glue it to the wall, then hang a braided bread wreath over it. The counter is placed in front.

22 | Among the accessories, you can make: a firewood basket from twine glued onto a slice of a Christmas ball ornament, fabric flour sacks, a twig broom, and miller's clogs from peanut shells to hang on the wall. The LED light string's battery pack is hidden upstairs; the lights run along the top of the right wall and under the front roof, reach the center of the room in the lampshade, and end behind the upper window.

THE SCRIBBLE SPIRAL

MATERIALS

box: recycled cardboard

—

lighting: none

—

craft materials: white paper, thin wooden skewers, straws

—

tools: fine black marker (0.3 mm), thicker black marker for coloring, pencil, eraser, ruler, craft knife, scissors, clear tape, awl or other pointed tool

Drawing

Lose track of time by doodling endlessly until you reach the feeling of timelessness in the eye of the cyclone. This is the concept proposed by illustrator Léo Allain, who was invited to create this dizzying book nook.

1 | Prepare eight paper rectangles measuring approximately 4 x 10¼ inches (10 x 26 cm). Use a pencil to draw ½-inch (1-cm) strips at the top and bottom of each page to serve as folding tabs. The detailed pattern areas should form a ring 1¼-inch (3-cm) wide around the hole. Beyond that, it can be colored in black.

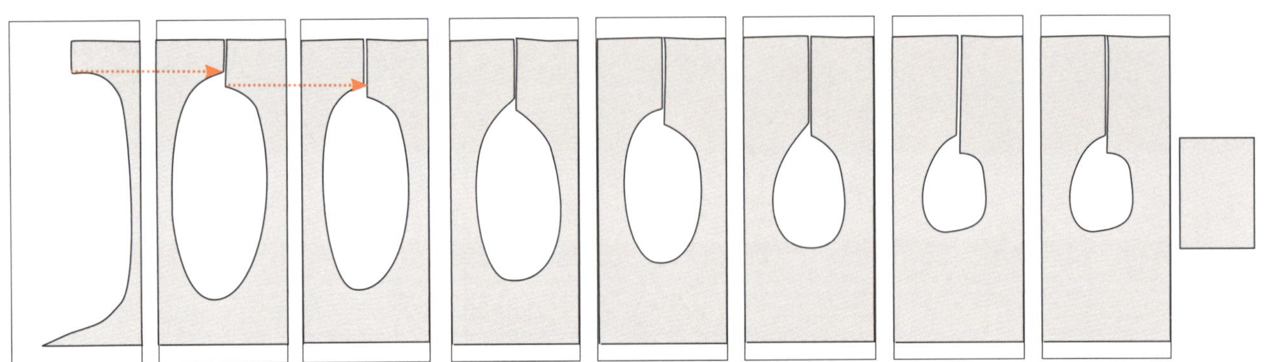

2 | Draw half an oval on the right side of the first sheet and doodle freely in the area between the oval and the edge, as you might do absentmindedly during a phone call.

3 | Cut out this half band and align it with the second rectangle to continue the drawing seamlessly, making the oval slightly narrower. Be careful not to smudge the ink while working.

4 | Continue in this manner until you reach the last sheet. The central hole will gradually shrink with each layer. Outside the ring of doodles, color everything to the edge black, as this area will be less visible.

5 | Cut out the shapes.

Assembly

6 | Tape wooden skewers measuring 9½ inches (24 cm) along the long sides of each paper rectangle. Fold the top and bottom tabs over like hems, inserting skewers measuring 3½ inches (9 cm) long into the top fold.

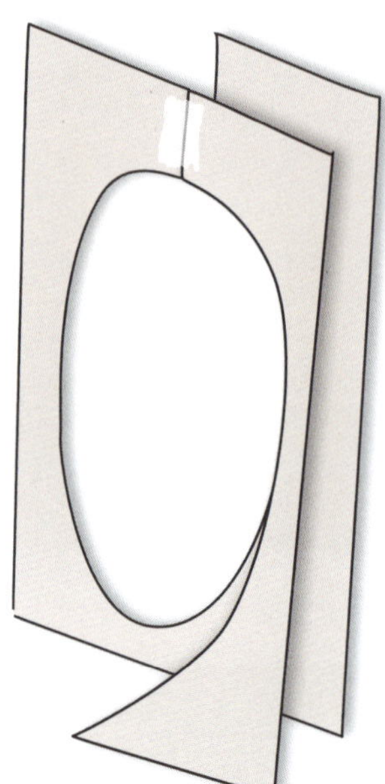

7 | Assemble the pieces following the diagram: line up the first strip at the top with the notch in the second sheet, whose right side is then taped to the left side of the next one, and so on for all eight panels.

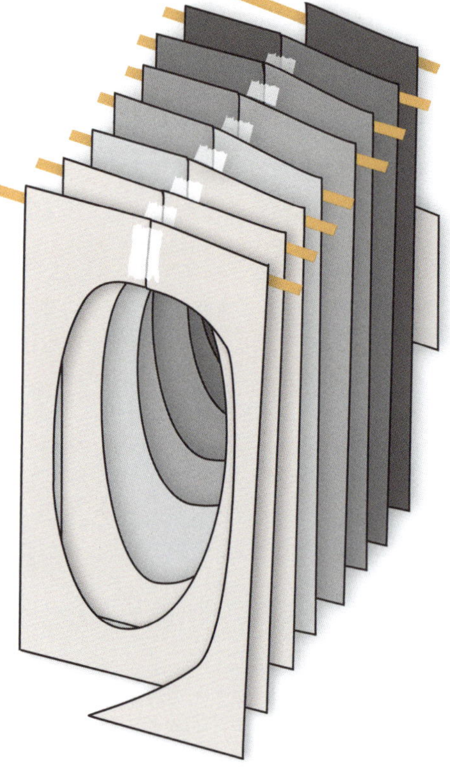

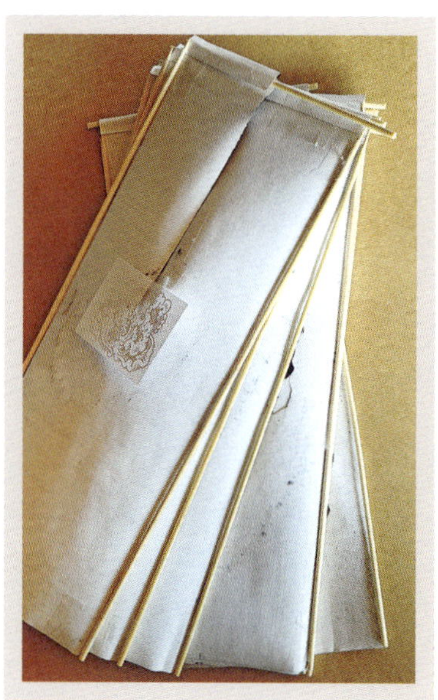

8 | Finally, place a small drawing over the last hole. The sheets are now suspended as if on hangers, ready to be mounted inside a fitted box. The horizontal skewer system allows you to adjust the spacing between sheets to create the desired depth.

Finalizing the Box

9 | Cut sturdy cardboard to create a box that fits the size of the drawings, approximately 3 inches (8 cm) wide, 9½ inches (24 cm) high, and 10 inches (25 cm) deep.

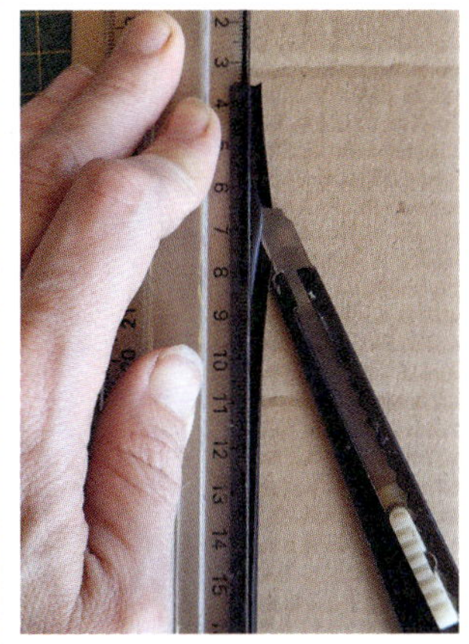

10 | Use a craft knife to slit black straws lengthwise while holding them steady under a flat ruler.

11 | Punch holes in the straws every 1 inch (2.5 cm), then thread and glue them along the edges of the cardboard. Insert the panels' skewers into the holes in order to space them evenly.

12 | There is no artificial lighting in this book nook as the effect comes from the depth of the spiral, with its increasingly dark center creating an illusion of infinity. To explore more artwork in this style, visit Allain's Instagram account, aptly named Gris Bouillis (a play on the French word *scribouiller*, which means "to scribble").

THE ARTIST'S STUDIO

MATERIALS

box: beautiful wooden frame with glass, MDF boards, wooden sticks or skewers

—

lighting: thin string of LED lights and ultraflat LED coaster light, both battery-operated

—

to find: photo of the streets of Montmartre, bust of a very small doll or figurine

—

small materials: various bottle caps, colored straws (including one black), pushpins, paper clips, pencil with an eraser, white thread, twine, black cord, thin wire, black tape, glitter, small nails, short pins, candle, matches, craft sticks, stir sticks, wooden skewers, toothpicks, glue, paint, black ink

—

craft materials: air-drying modeling clay; plaster; cardboard; wallpaper; green, red, and gold tissue paper; white fabric

—

tools: saw, hammer, sandpaper, drill, 1⅜-inch (35-mm) spade drill bit, scissors, craft knife, glue gun, paintbrush, needle, fine-tipped pliers

The Box

THE KEY FEATURE OF THIS BOOK NOOK IS A FRAME IN THE FOREGROUND, WITH ITS GLASS PLACED AT AN ANGLE IN THE BACKGROUND TO CREATE A STUDIO SKYLIGHT OVERLOOKING A PHOTOGRAPHIC VIEW OF THE PARIS ROOFTOPS. IT INCORPORATES DUAL LIGHTING FOR BOTH THE INDOOR AND OUTDOOR SECTIONS.

1 | Determine the dimensions for the box based on the frame. Remove its back panel.

2 | Cut the five wooden panels needed to form the box.

3 | Glue two wooden strips to the base to align the floor with the frame's height. Mark the ceiling placement and nail two wooden strips diagonally on the walls to support the glass.

4 | Attach the ceiling, left wall, and floor. Build a small supporting wall for the skylight with a shelf on top. Apply black adhesive strips to the glass.

5 | Drill a 1⅜-inch (35-mm) hole in the ceiling to insert the LED coaster light.

6 | Print or develop a photo to be placed at the back, including triangular side extensions. You can push the detail further and glue moss to the sidewalls if it would enhance the photo. Paint the walls white, the floor black, and a light blue sky above the photo.

The Furniture

7 | The stove is made from two cut and assembled metal bottle caps wrapped in black tape. The pipe is a bent straw.

8 | For the inside, create flames using gold gift wrap and red tissue paper, inserted into a cardboard base. Make a hole in the back for lighting. Assemble and attach pushpin legs.

9 | Cut craft sticks (or other thin wood strips) to assemble two identical frames. Glue them together to form two trestles and place a flat strip on top. Add a thin loop of wire and position the tabletop on top.

10 | Glue the easel together using wooden stir sticks following this model.

11 | The stool consists of a slice of cork glued onto cut skewer legs reinforced with matchsticks, then splattered with paint.

Accessories

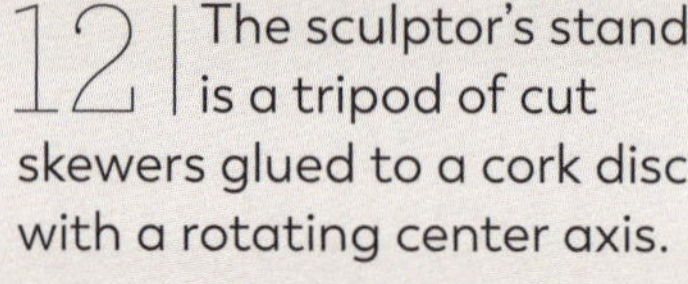

12 | The sculptor's stand is a tripod of cut skewers glued to a cork disc with a rotating center axis.

13 | To create the sculpture bust, dip a small doll's torso in plaster.

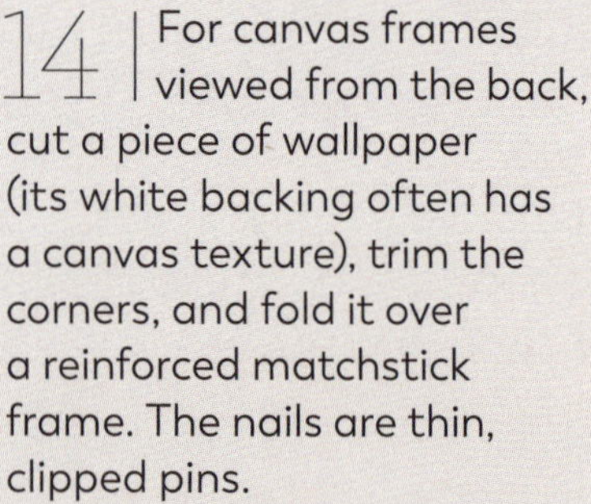

14 | For canvas frames viewed from the back, cut a piece of wallpaper (its white backing often has a canvas texture), trim the corners, and fold it over a reinforced matchstick frame. The nails are thin, clipped pins.

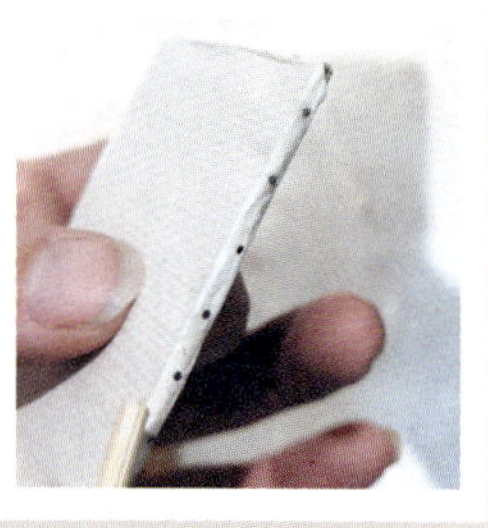

15 | A brush is made by sticking twine through the ink tube of a ballpoint pen. The pencils are toothpicks. The pot can be either a covered piece of a straw or a pencil eraser cap.

16 | A simplified version of upright canvases when you only see the front: cardboard covered with paper and nails drawn on the edges.

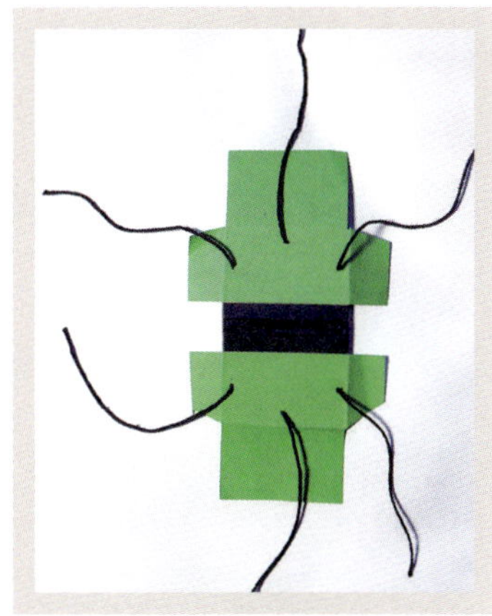

17 | For the portfolio, cut two rectangles of cardboard, wrap them in green paper as shown, connect them with black fabric tape. Punch out tiny holes, thread them with black string, tape the ends on the back, and glue the green flaps over top.

18 | Splatter black ink on the portfolio by rubbing a small brush over a match. Attach two stir sticks to the left wall as a shelf to hold the portfolio.

19 | Sew a small apron with a pocket. Cut out a cardboard palette.

20 | Sew a simple smock following this pattern. Gather the neckline and add splatters of paint.

21 | Bend a paper clip into a hanger.

22 | Fray twine and tie it to a cut skewer to create a broom.

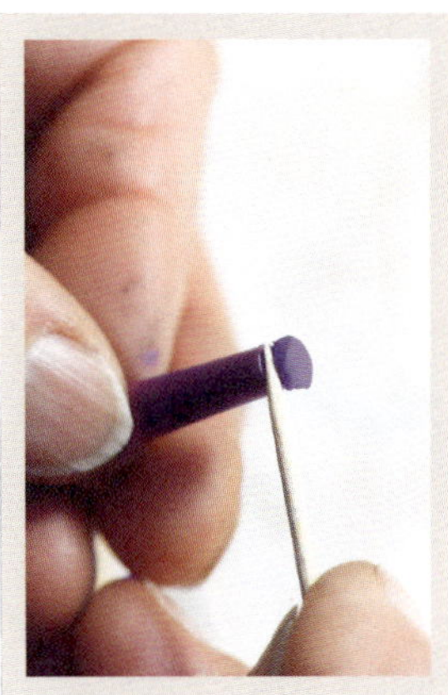

23 | To make miniature paint tubes, pinch the end of a plastic straw with pliers that have been heated over a candle.

24 | Cut the other end with scissors, then insert the tube into modeling clay to fill it and shape the cap.

You can even use the bent part of a bendy straw to make a twisted paint tube.

Lighting

25 | This book nook features two lighting modes. The first is an LED coaster light mounted at the top behind the glass.

26 | This emits a white light—giving the illusion of moonlight behind the skylight.

27 | To light the studio itself, fix the string light's battery pack behind the frame on the bottom right. Insert the first two LED bulbs into the stove from behind, then loop back along the frame to the ceiling. Place a special picture light in the middle of the right wall.

28 | The remaining lights coil around a white pushpin in the center of the room, forming a ceiling fixture made from a small bottle cap (here, a contact lens solution cap). This setup allows you to light the exterior, interior, or both.

Fruits

THE EXPANDING STREET

MATERIALS

structure: large sturdy cardboard box

—

lighting: thin string of LED lights 4 to 6 feet (2 to 3 meters) long with button cell batteries

—

craft materials: papers in various colors and textures, brick-patterned wallpaper or scrapbook paper, tissue paper, assorted cardboard scraps, especially honeycomb board, fiber fill or cotton balls, sand, window screen, cork

—

to gather: small cardboard packages (medicine boxes, matchboxes, cookie boxes), transparent plastic packages (trays), catalogues, small crates, dried flowers and lichen

—

to repurpose: skewer stick, craft sticks, straws, paper cupcake liners, holiday garland, fruit slice nail decorations, small suction cup hook, pendant for a sign

—

small materials: beads, wire, matches, paint, walnut stain (or ink), coarse sandpaper, tape, chalk, white marker, black Micron pen

—

tools: various decorative hole punches, scissors, craft knife, glue gun, paintbrush, precision pliers, awl

THIS BOOK NOOK CAN BE POSITIONED IN TWO WAYS: OPEN OR FOLDED. A STREET MADE FROM RECYCLED PACKAGING, WITH THE HELP OF DECORATIVE PUNCHES.

The Composition

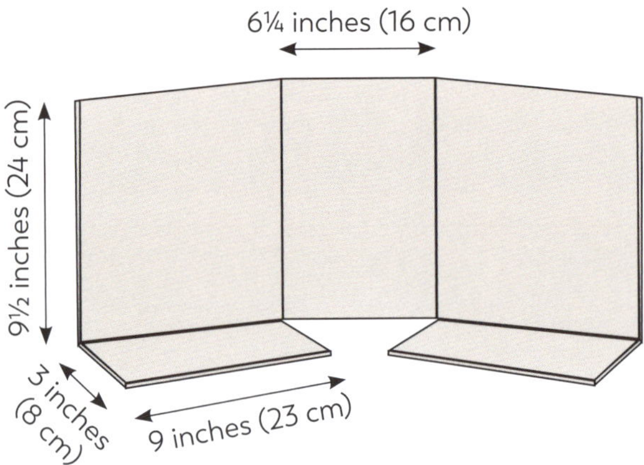

1 | Cut and assemble a sturdy box cardboard to create a shape like this, which will serve as the base.

2 | Turn the small boxes inside out. Experiment with different combinations, keeping in mind the folding constraints.

3 | The left side features a series of slightly angled facades, with a narrow building in the foreground when closed (thus on the left) and a deeper house on the right, set away from the back, allowing another building (in red) to fit into the back corner.

4 | On the right side, the composition is guided by a cookie box spanning the entire width of the upper floor, on which three small matchboxes are placed. Below, there is a shop in the back (when closed, on the left), a recessed area in the middle, and a shallow house in the foreground (on the right).

The Buildings on the Right Side

5 | Cut a long rectangle out of an inside-out cookie box to insert a transparent checkered plastic tray (herb packaging).

6 | Glue a background paper inside, then cut out plants from a store catalogue to simulate a veranda.

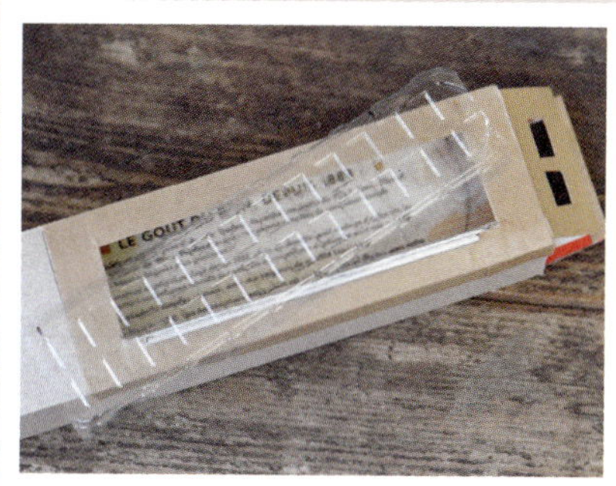

7 | Outline the window frames in white marker and paint the facade blue. (For a weathered look, first cover with beige tape with a slightly plasticized finish, which makes the paint easy to chip off.) Attach a canopy made of a cut white cupcake liner.

8 | The shop is painted green and black, with pencil strokes drawn into the paint to mimic wood planks.

9 | The red awning is perforated with a decorative punch. Add a small counter and a doorstep made of thin strips of wood.

10 | This thin cardboard window has corners at an angle to give it depth. It will be fit into a box.

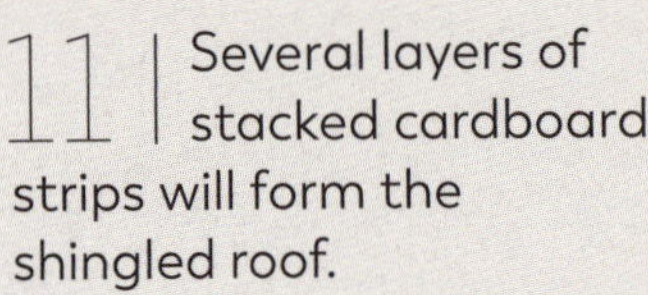

11 | Several layers of stacked cardboard strips will form the shingled roof.

12 | Paint the pieces before gluing them together, leaving an opening in the back for the string of LED lights.

13 | Cut the two sides for the steps from foam board. Glue crate slats as steps and stain with diluted ink.

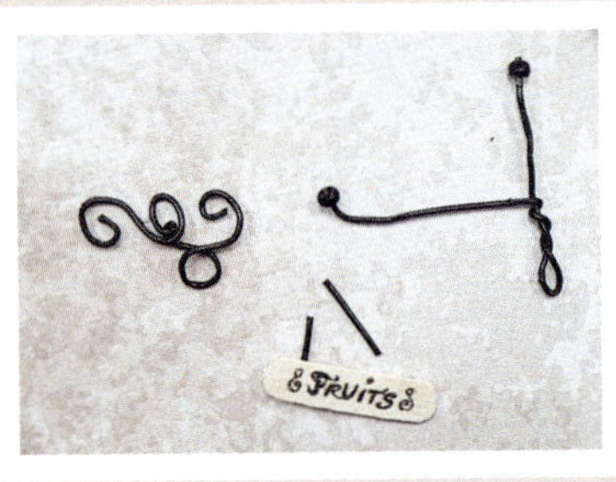

14 | Create the shop sign with thin, flexible black wire. Attach seed beads at the ends. Write the shop's name on a small piece of wood using a Micron pen. Attach the sign to the facade. Assemble the lower level elements and cover them with a corrugated cardboard roof (peeling off a layer of cardboard reveals the inner texture).

15 | The upper floor consists of three small matchboxes covered with paper perforated with a decorative punch. The middle box is adorned with a piece of red fringe from a holiday garland, and its canopy rests on two matches. The box on the right has tissue paper curtains. Remember to make holes in the back to allow the lighting to pass through.

16 | For the planter, trim the bottom of a juice box, cut out leaves with a decorative punch, and glue them onto small pieces of wire. Attach them to a base of green tissue paper.

17 | The clothesline is made of wire, with tissue paper clothes glued onto it.

18 | In front of the produce stand, the crates on the ground are made of small pieces of matchsticks. On a bed of green tissue paper, alternate small balls of colored modeling clay and miniature polymer clay fruit slices, originally sold as nail decorations.

19 | By dismantling a necklace that was bought secondhand, a large bead and some decorative elements can be salvaged to create a streetlamp. The base is a black straw. The large bead is secured with a star-shaped wire, which runs through the straw and is glued to the ground.

20 | To add a humorous and realistic touch: some dog poop can be painted onto a glass surface, peeled off with a craft knife, and carefully glued at the foot of the streetlamp with a few small pebbles.

21 | In the foreground, a small, perforated paper lantern sits under a corolla-shaped bead with a wire handle passing through it. Another wire, twisted into an arabesque shape, serves as a support. Now, all that is needed is the lighting.

The Left Side

22 | To create the central building, unfold a cookie box, cut arches into the upper floor with a craft knife, line the inside with decorative paper, and close the box inside out. The gate is made of wood (craft sticks, crate slats, or old blinds) glued to a thin cardboard backing and stained with diluted walnut stain (or ink). Draw the wall stones with a pencil and chalk (ocher and white).

23 | Above the doorway, attach a small suction cup hook, already perforated with a nail. Its shape suggests an outdoor wall sconce. One of the LED bulbs will pass through it to create the illusion.

24 | The roof will be made from a piece of cork, but it will be cut later to adjust it to the oblique alignment of the building facades.

25 | A cookie box with a pointed top forms the right-side house, covered with wood-patterned paper and decorated with windows. The roof is made of corrugated cardboard.

26 | For the pointed house, add a chimney with cotton smoke and a small raised walkway at its base.

27 | This slim box inspired the design of tall, narrow windows lined with a piece of window screen inside. Since it is on a small scale, this building will be placed in the back. It will be attached to a wooden skewer glued behind the pointed house, which sits slightly further out into the street to free up space in the corner.

28 | The small market stand on the left is topped with a terrace, whose railing is cut with a decorative punch and glued onto the outside of a piece of beige tape. The stall is made of craft sticks. Some foliage hides the electrical wire in the corner.

29 | Another way to make a sign: use a pendant with a small paper panel hanging from it.

30 | Two types of punches were used to make the flower arrangements: one flower-shaped and the other leaf-shaped. Small pins were inserted into vases made from sections of drinking straws, and then some spherical, colorful pushpins were added. These pots are placed in the foreground to add vibrancy.

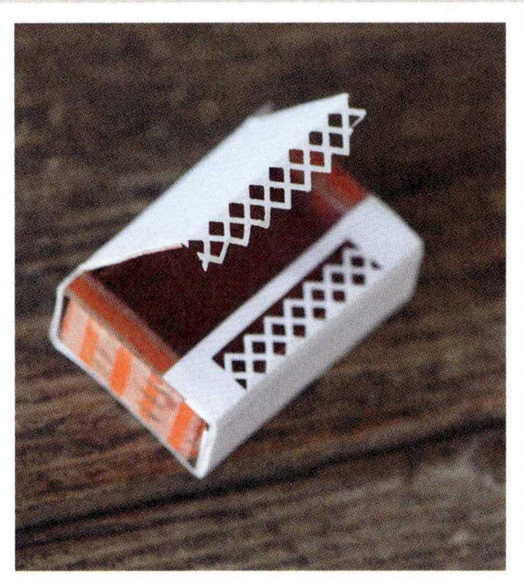

31 | Three other matchboxes are covered with perforated paper but stacked vertically this time. They will be glued in the back above the shop's terrace roof.

Assembly and Lighting

32 | Crumple gray tissue paper, then flatten it on a coarse piece of sandpaper. Rub white chalk over it to create a textured print resembling asphalt, then glue it to the floor on both sides of the support structure.

33 | Line the inside wall of the structure with textured paper and the outside with brick-patterned wallpaper. Glue all of the buildings and the streetlamp in place, as well as the vegetation behind the left-side walls.

34 | Add final details: a straw downspout and some sand, gravel, or foliage in the corners. Create a small cover for the electrical battery box.

35 | Here is the wiring plan for the string of LED lights. This step is quite long and fiddly but is made easier if you have prepunched holes in the back of the boxes. The starting point is on the left, and the final light ends in the right-side lantern. The wire should be as discreet as possible. In the central passage, it is hidden under a paper flap; between the small boxes on the right, a few clouds of cotton conceal it.

BIG BAD CITY
Akiko Ida / Pierre Javelle
Le jardin des Minimiams
ARTISANS
NOUVELLES TENDANCES

Rêves
MICROCOSMOS
LE PEUPLE DE L'HERBE
Claude Nuridsany et Marie Pérennou
Éditions de La Martinière
Hocus Pocus
Elzbieta
ROUERGUE
PRÉDICTIONS
les moindres petites choses
anne herbauts
casterman
CONSTRUIRE DES CABANES EN BOIS
CURIOSA
A
LE CHÂTEAU SUSPENDU
PHILEMON
DARGAUD
LA POÉSIE POPULAIRE
Autels intimes
Tana
E
LE PIANO SAUVAGE
PHILEMON
DARGAUD
N
LE VOYAGE DE L'INCRÉDULE
PHILEMON
DARGAUD

THE TREE HOUSE ON WATER

MATERIALS

box: reclaimed plywood painted white

—

lighting: a thin string of LED lights with button cell batteries and another with ten "stick" LEDs powered by AAA batteries

—

about 18 ounces (500 g) of transparent melt-and-pour soap

—

dried green plant with beautiful roots (pictured: bonsai ficus)

—

small branch of dried green flowers

—

drink carton with a square base (from juice, for example)

—

small materials: wooden crate slats, twine, toothpicks, blue ink cartridge, white clay, colored nail polish

—

tools: craft knife, glue gun, fine screwdriver, jigsaw

GIVE A SECOND LIFE TO A DEAD PLANT AND MIMIC RESIN . . . WITH SOAP.

Build the Tree House

2 | Cut slats from a crate and assemble them to form the three visible walls of a cabin (front side pictured above, back below).

3 | Cut out the roof. Cover it with tiny shingles glued in an overlapping pattern.

4 | Cut out the terrace (3 inches or 8 cm max), make holes along the edge, insert cut toothpicks, and weave twine through them.

1 | Strip the roots of the plant.

5 | Arrange the string of lights so that the LED bulbs extend under the roof. Keep some slack in the back.

Molding the Block of Water

6 | Melt the soap in a double boiler. Pour it into a drink carton cut two-thirds of the way down. Pour in the contents of a blue ink cartridge and mix. Submerge the roots in the mixture.

7 | Once the block has solidified, cut open the carton. Glue the cabin on top of the roots, then attach the dried flowers on the top of the house.

8 | Use a screwdriver to drill some deep holes in the back of the soap block and insert the large ends of the LED stick lights.

10 | Tint the LED bulbs with nail polish. Whiten any cracks and edges on the house with clay.

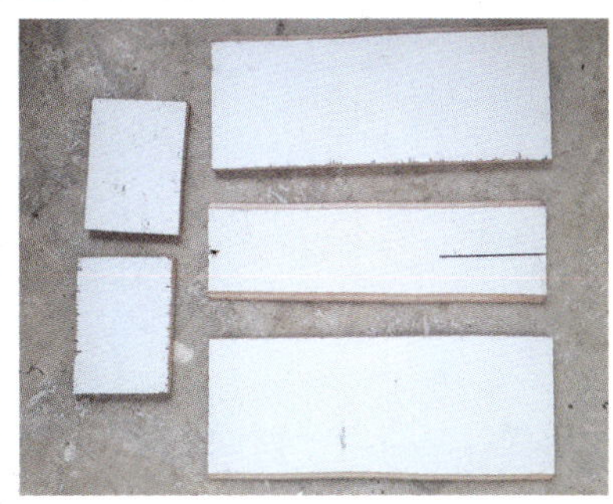

9 | Use a jigsaw to cut pieces of plywood to create a fitted box. Leave space at the back but not on the sides. Make two notches in the bottom for the cables to pass through. Glue the battery packs in place.

GONE WITH THE WIND
GABRIEL GARCIA MARQUEZ 100 YEARS OF SOLITUDE

THE LIBRARY

MATERIALS

box: thick cardboard

lighting: two thin strings of LED lights with button cell batteries

to gather: mini book covers to print or cut out, dollhouse bottles, plastic deer head (from a Christmas ornament), small piece of rose quartz

craft materials: cardboard, foam board, air-dry clay, colored modeling clay, crate wood, white paper, patterned paper, green tissue paper, gold paper, twigs, ash, small red pebbles, patterned fabric, felt

small supplies: paint, beads, small nails, ribbons, lace, fine wire, glue, string, cork, wooden stir sticks, small tacks, candle, straws

tools: scissors, craft knife, hot glue gun, ruler, decorative pinking shears, paintbrush, small rotary multitool

The Frame

A TINY LIBRARY TO SLIP INTO YOUR LARGER ONE. TO MAKE THE ILLUSION COMPLETE, YOU CAN HAVE FUN PHOTOGRAPHING AND REPRODUCING THE BOOKS YOU HAVE AT HOME.

1 | Create or repurpose a sturdy cardboard box. The one in the photo is 7 inches (18 cm) wide, 7½ inches (19 cm) deep, and 10½ inches (27 cm) high. Attach ¾-inch (2-cm) wide shelves inside.

2 | Paint the shelves and cover their edges with string to hide the thickness of the cardboard. Keep in mind that the more shelves there are, the more books you will need to fill them! Shape a frame out of cardboard covered with air-dry clay. Carve stonelike patterns into it.

3 | Cover the floor with thin wooden crate slats to imitate a wood floor. Paint it.

4 | Craft a chandelier using three bulbs from the string of LED lights and three wire spirals decorated with beads.

The Decor

5 | Cover the walls with patterned paper that mimics wallpaper.

6 | Shape the fireplace using cardboard covered with air-dry clay. Etch a brick-like pattern into it. Paint it in multiple layers after drying. To create the fire, glue together small twigs, a few transparent red pebbles, and flames made from gold paper.

7 | To create a vintage-style frame, cut a rectangle from cardboard and cut a smaller rectangle in its center. Cover it with gold paper (from a chocolate wrapper) and glue it in place. Make an X-shaped cut in the smaller opening and fold back the four triangular flaps, covering the inner edges of the cardboard frame. Use decorative pinking shears to shape the edges and place a mirror or portrait in the center.

8 | To make a small lamp to place on the fireplace, glue a tubular bead onto a round bead (large enough for the LED string to pass through). Cut an arc-shaped piece from patterned paper, glue it into a lampshade shape, and place it on the base.

Lighting and Furnishings

9 | Install the lighting: the battery pack is hidden behind the frame on the left. The wiring runs through the wall to light up the inside of the fireplace, then the lamp placed on top. The string then runs under the lowest shelf, exits to illuminate a rose quartz stone glued in place like a Himalayan salt lamp, continues to the front, rises up to the right to light up the liquor bottles, then the plant above, and finally ends among the books.

10 | The armchair and table are made of cardboard covered with fabric, then decorated with beads and ribbons. The wooden legs are glued on.

11 | The firewood crate is made from glued-together slats of a wooden crate, then painted black. It is filled with a bundle of twigs.

12 | To make the plant, cut strips of green tissue paper into pointed shapes. Fold them in half and glue them onto pieces of thin wire. Stick the leaves into a champagne cork cut to the right height and partially painted black.

13 | The fireplace accessories are made of wire; the brush is made from string fibers. The shovel is a fork with its prongs connected by tissue paper.

14 | The rug is a piece of wide canvas ribbon (jute) with frayed edges. The kitten, made of air-dry clay, has black seed bead eyes. The rest of the face was drawn after drying with a fine-tip Micron pen.

15 | To make the cat's basket, glue together two layers of foam board cut into a bean shape. Insert small, slightly wide-headed nails into it. Wrap string around the nails in a woven pattern. Cover the base with ribbon and place a felt mat inside.

16 | The deer head was salvaged from a broken Christmas ornament. The angle of its neck was adjusted using a small circular saw (this can also be done with a metal saw or even a serrated knife). The frame is made of modeling clay. Once hardened, it can be glued to the wall with a hot glue gun.

On the Shelves

17 | To make the vases, you can fill wooden beads (the white ones are made from clay) with dried plant sprigs. These will help create some variety with the books and keep them upright.

18 | Keep an eye out for other miniature objects, like this small balance weight that resembles a jar, that work as bookends.

19 | Wooden beads glued onto two pieces of a stir stick make bookends that will punctuate the shelves of the library.

20 | The candles are made like real ones. Cut small sections of drinking straws. Close the bottoms with some modeling clay. Insert a small piece of kitchen twine inside. Light a candle and let the wax drip into the tubes. Once it hardens, split open the straw to remove the candle and glue it onto a small cylindrical bead.

The Books

21 | Making the little books is the central aspect of this project. To fill the library shown in the photo, 165 books had to be made! You can find digital files of mini book covers for sale on Etsy to print, or you can make them yourself—for example, by photographing your own library. Alternatively, you can cut out images from publishers' catalogues. There are three options for making the pages: dismantling a book and cutting small bundles from the already glued spine; creating paper accordion folds and gluing them; or covering small rectangles of foam board (you will not see the pages, but it creates neat volumes).

FASTKING
Arabian Nights

Volvic
MAYONNAISE
Fine
SEL
POIVRE

THE LITTLE RETRO KITCHEN

MATERIALS

box: recycled cardboard

—

lighting: thin string of LED lights with button cell batteries

—

to repurpose: small metal candy or mint container, corks, plastic caps, straw, toothbrush, oval paper box, chocolate box, flat game pieces, ballpoint pen, pencil with an eraser, eggshells, Christmas ornaments, pebble, foam bumper pads, eye dropper, pill bottles, catalogue, blue buttons, soda can, sardine tin, bottle caps, crate, craft sticks, wooden stir sticks, chopsticks, skewers, matches, toothpicks

—

small materials: tissue paper, patterned paper, aluminum foil, parchment paper, pushpins (wooden, flat metal, and round plastic), thread, string, wire, modeling clay, nail polish, candle, glue, paint, markers, glitter, beads, ribbons

—

tools: scissors, craft knife, pliers, nail file, pen tip, needle, paintbrush, hot glue gun

The Countertop

A VIBRANT VINTAGE KITCHEN WHOSE CHARM LIES IN THE METICULOUS DETAILS. THE CHALLENGE? REPURPOSING AS MANY EVERYDAY OBJECTS AS POSSIBLE.

1 | Create the counter using thick cardboard, the width of the box chosen, with a recess cut into it for the sink.

2 | Create the small sink by gluing together crate slats, lined with aluminum foil. Glue it into the hole.

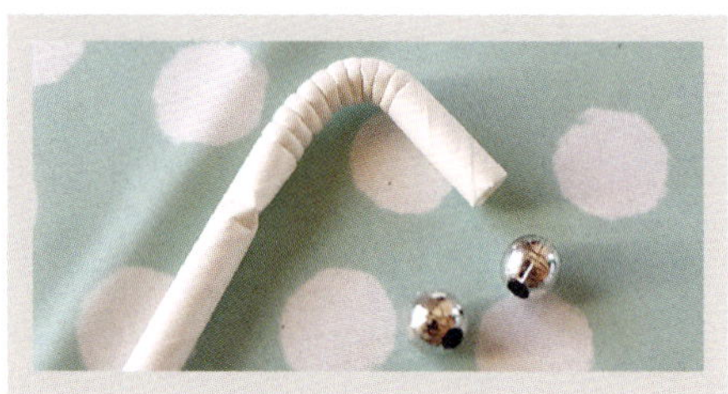

3 | To make the faucet, combine a small straw from a juice box and two silver beads.

4 | Cover the countertop with the crate slats, adding an extra layer where the doors are located. Paint them. Glue round bead handles or pairs of beads connected by a toothpick wrapped in aluminum.

5 | To make the gas stove, cover a small cardboard rectangle with a piece of metal cut from a can and glue on two blue buttons with black wire threaded through them. Two pushpins serve as the buttons.

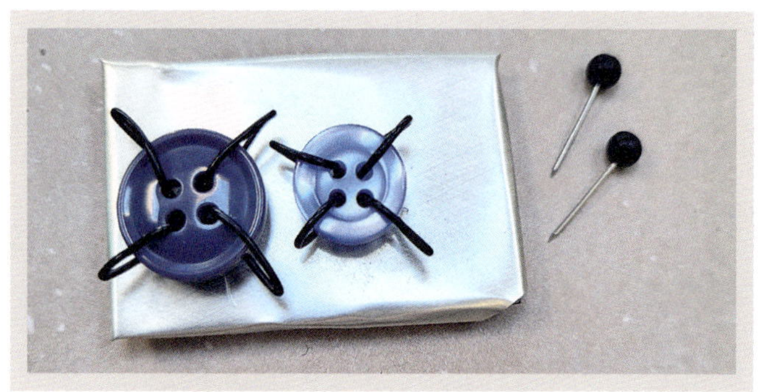

The Shelf and the Water Heater

6 | For the water heater, remove the label from a small candy tin with a sliding lid. Use seed beads for buttons and a piece of bendy straw for the ventilation pipe.

7 | Create the wall shelf using slats from a crate, wide enough to fit above the counter based on the size of the water heater. Glue the pieces together with a hot glue gun and paint them white.

8 | Fold a strip of white paper to create plate rack compartments and glue it into one of the sections of the shelf. The red plates in the photo are repurposed pieces from a board game.

The Tin Cans

9 | Cut the metal crown off the end of a pencil eraser. The eraser can serve as a garnish (e.g., red) or you can make something from modeling clay (e.g., green). Glue on a lid cut from the metal of a can (use pinking shears if you are aiming for extra detail).

The Back Wall

10 | To create the backsplash, cut a piece of thin cardboard to the length of the counter and paint it red. Coat it with white glue (invisible once dry), then crush white eggshell fragments with your fingers to create a faux mosaic tile pattern. (This Japanese art is called *rankaku.*)

11 | A bottle cap, a button, a section of a straw, and voilà—the base for a beautiful pie, which you can create using colored polymer clay or air-drying clay, ready to be painted.

12 | Glue the backsplash in place, then add a simple shelf made from a crate slat painted white. Next, glue floral-print paper up to the ceiling, then attach the shelf and the water heater. Below the cooktop, a wire support holds some dish towels.

13 | To make the saltshaker and pepper mill, use two pushpins and write on them with an ultrafine Micron pen.

The Jars

14 | To make the miniature jars, cut sections of hot glue sticks (¼ inch or 7 mm) with a craft knife. For a clean cut, heat the blade.

15 | Round off the edges of the tops so that the width of the sticks tapers up to the metal pushpins that will be pressed into them as lids.

16 | Cut labels from a grocery store flyer and glue them onto the jars.

17 | Another way to make jars is by cutting an old ballpoint pen with a serrated knife or hacksaw. The tip, decorated with a bead, can serve as a small bottle. The other end of the pen already has its plastic lid.

The Small Utensils

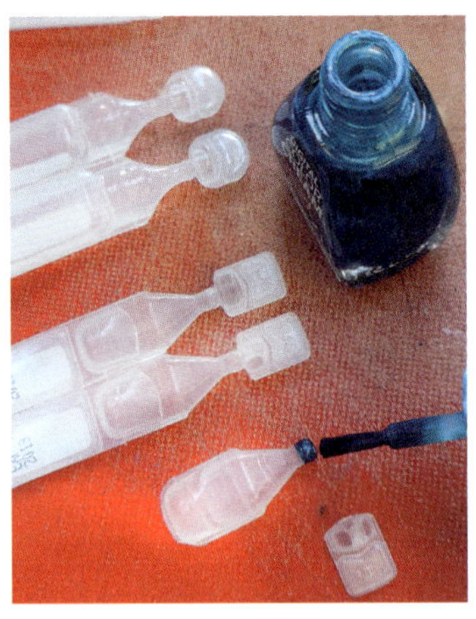

18 | A simple way to make mini bottles is by repurposing plastic eye droppers. Cut off the part that looks like a bottle and dab a bit of nail polish on top: its slight thickness will resemble a colored cork. Cut a label from a flyer.

19 | This entire gold set was cut out from the packaging of a holiday chocolate box. The molded shapes were cleverly used to create plates, cutlery, dishes, and lids.

20 | A quick look through your medicine cabinets can uncover treasures in used pill blister packs: small white or translucent plastic bowls.

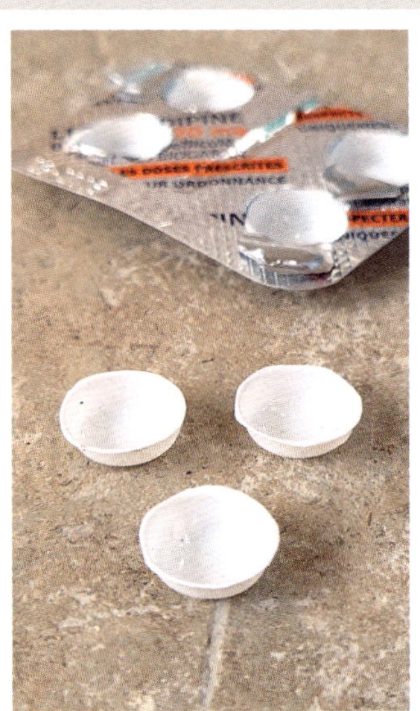

23 | Spatulas can be cut with a craft knife from pieces of crate wood.

24 | In the sink, the orange modeling clay carrots are adorned with greens cut from paper using a decorative punch. These can be found in a craft store with scrapbook supplies. The lettuce is a strip of green tissue paper cut into a garland of leaves, rolled up, and gathered at the base.

21 | Other metallic pill packaging can be used to create all sorts of containers with the appearance of aluminum or stainless steel, such as a strainer (on its three little feet), a wok, or a lid.

22 | To make a stockpot, all that was needed for this lid was a bottle top covered in silver (with a marker or spray paint).

The Left Wall

25 | To make the blind, cut a piece of white paper and fold it accordion-style every ¼ inch (5 mm). A trick for even folding: mark the folds with the back of a craft knife, alternating one on the front and the others on the back. Thread two strings through it using a needle. Glue the blind onto a frame made from craft sticks with tracing paper at the back. You can add a perpendicular stir stick as a window sill with a bead vase and a sprig of dried flowers.

26 | The chair is made from a painted bottle cap with four wire legs adorned with seed beads and a backrest made from a pull tab.

27 | The chandelier is a Christmas ornament cut in half and covered in string. A string of LEDs is held inside by a transparent plastic wall cut from a blister pack. The switch is attached on the top of the box.

28 | To make the table, cut the ends of four chopsticks with a good serrated knife and glue them inside an oblong loaf pan liner reinforced with a cardboard bottom.

The Accessories

29 | Small Christmas ornaments, cut in half, can be used as shells to create baskets or salad bowls: one half covered with glued string, the other painted black and decorated with a string handle.

30 | The small cutting board is cut from a cork. The knife is made from the metal of a can, with brown nail polish on the handle and a sequin glued to it before it dries. You can make the fine kiwi slices yourself using polymer clay, but they can also be found as nail decorations!

31 | By carving a piece of cork with a gouge, you get a small salad bowl in which the ends of matchsticks have been glued as red fruits.

32 | To make the basket, cover a pebble with parchment paper, wrap it in a jute ribbon coated with glue, and let it dry. Then remove it from the mold and cut it with scissors, then glue on a handle made of twisted string and fill it with clay potatoes.

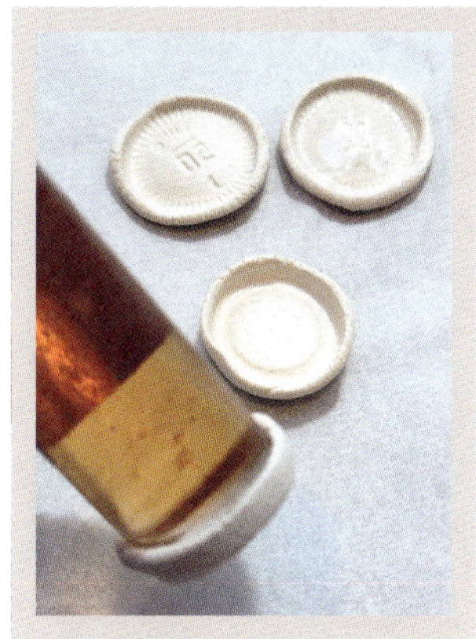

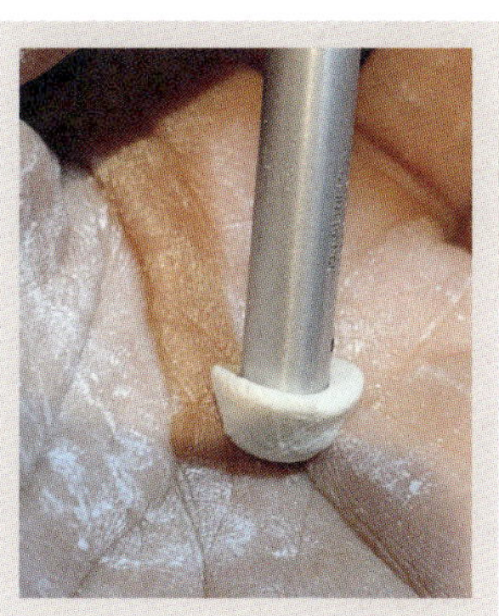

33 | To make plates, oil the bottoms of small bottles (perfume, essential oils, etc.), press a small piece of air-drying clay into them, then remove the clay and let them dry on parchment paper. To make cups or bowls, hollow out a small ball with a rounded tip and shape it in the hollow of your palm.

The Right Wall

34 | A vintage refrigerator model can be made from a sardine tin painted orange, with a handle made from medicine packaging.

35 | To make the paper towel dispenser, take a small piece of paper rolled and glued onto a toothpick, two pieces of twisted black wire shaped into arabesques, and carefully glue everything together using a fine-tip tube of precision glue.

36 | The broom is made from a cut toothbrush. To make the dustpan, heat the handle of the toothbrush over a candle, press it with pliers to shape it, and then cut it. Heat a piece of wire in the same way to pierce a plastic cap to use as a bucket and attach the handle. Then, pour some melted wax inside.

37 | The clock is a round of pins placed between two foam bumper pads. Then, add two hands cut from black paper and a sequin in the center.

38 | For the floor, use embossed paper with a grid pattern that resembles tiles. The rug in front of the sink is cut from a roll of fiber adhesive tape.

39 | The small cork bulletin board is made from two slices of cork glued together, framed with matchsticks.

Volvic
SEL
POIVRE
DENTISTE
courses
- tomates
- oignons
- farine
- gros sel

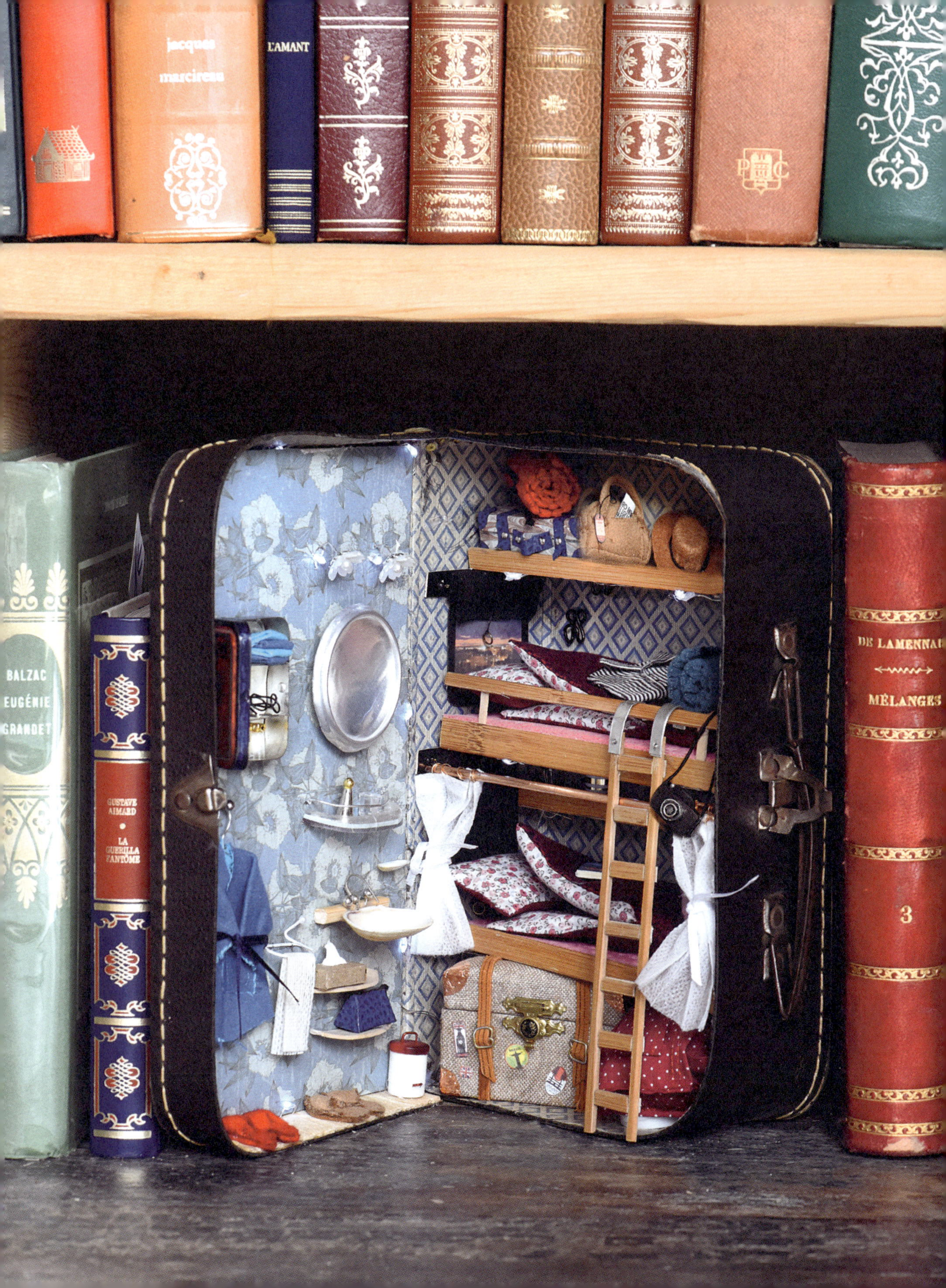
jacques
marcireau
L'AMANT
BALZAC
EUGÉNIE
GRANDET
GUSTAVE
AIMARD
LA
GUERILLA
FANTÔME
DE LAMENNAI
MÉLANGES
3

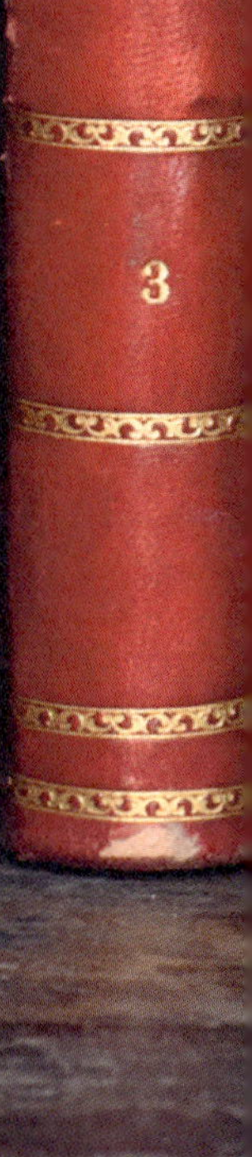

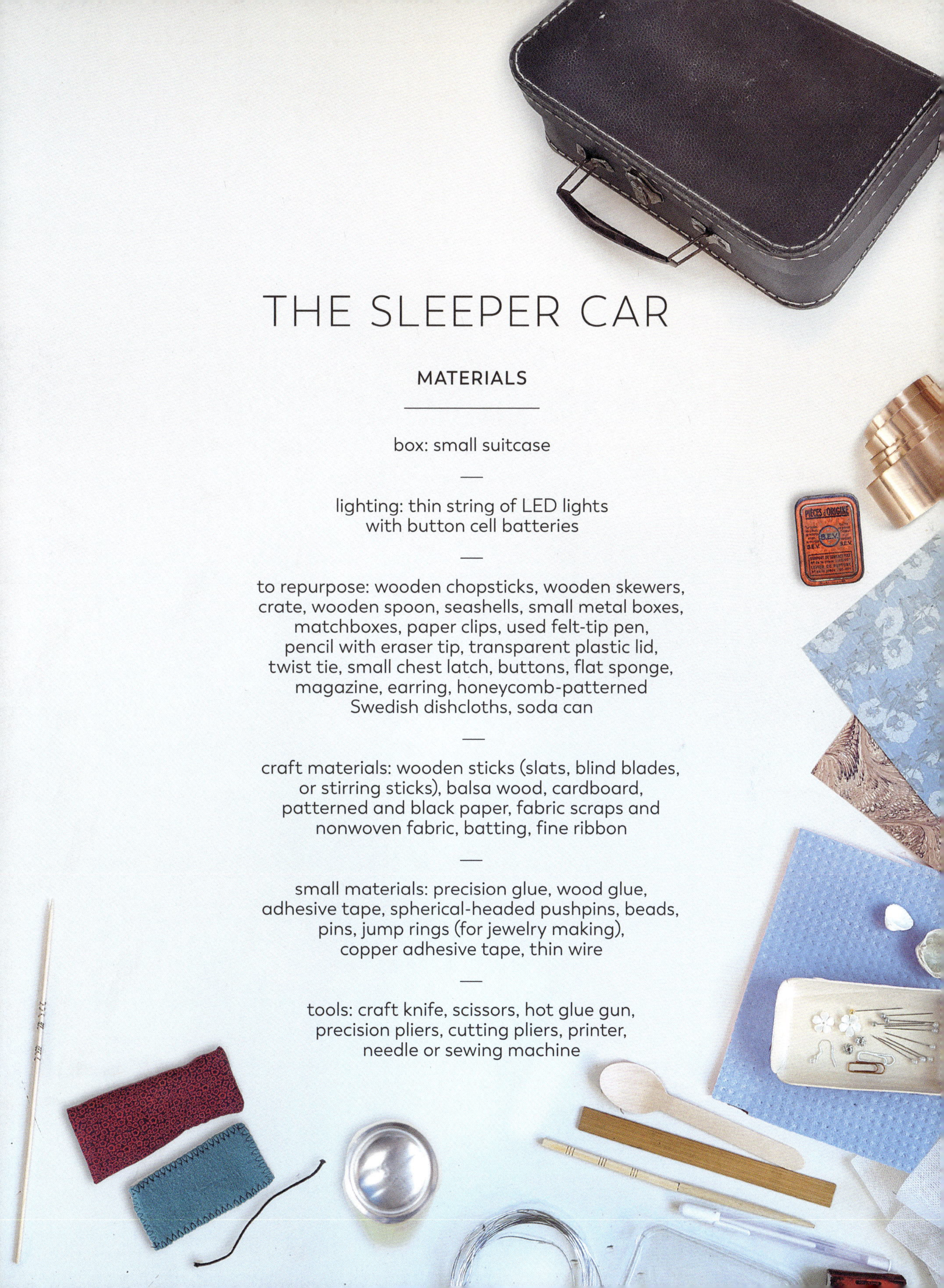

THE SLEEPER CAR

MATERIALS

box: small suitcase

—

lighting: thin string of LED lights with button cell batteries

—

to repurpose: wooden chopsticks, wooden skewers, crate, wooden spoon, seashells, small metal boxes, matchboxes, paper clips, used felt-tip pen, pencil with eraser tip, transparent plastic lid, twist tie, small chest latch, buttons, flat sponge, magazine, earring, honeycomb-patterned Swedish dishcloths, soda can

—

craft materials: wooden sticks (slats, blind blades, or stirring sticks), balsa wood, cardboard, patterned and black paper, fabric scraps and nonwoven fabric, batting, fine ribbon

—

small materials: precision glue, wood glue, adhesive tape, spherical-headed pushpins, beads, pins, jump rings (for jewelry making), copper adhesive tape, thin wire

—

tools: craft knife, scissors, hot glue gun, precision pliers, cutting pliers, printer, needle or sewing machine

The Bunk Beds

Choosing a small suitcase as a book nook case is already the start of a journey. This train cabin is filled with the cozy luxury of days gone by.

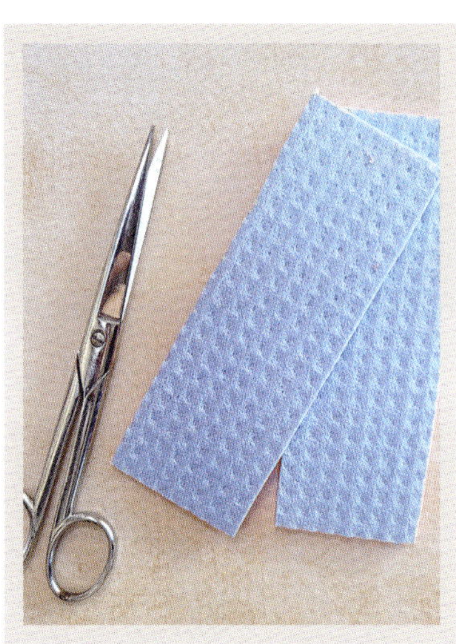

1 | Cut the bunk beds from cardboard measuring the width of the suitcase. Add a guardrail made of wooden slats.

2 | For the mattresses, a simple solution is to cut rectangles of honeycomb-patterned Swedish dishcloths.

3 | The luggage rack is made of wooden sticks without cardboard, along with a small safety bar.

4 | To give the bar an antique and luxurious look, it can be covered with copper-effect adhesive tape. You could also use a metallic paint or pen.

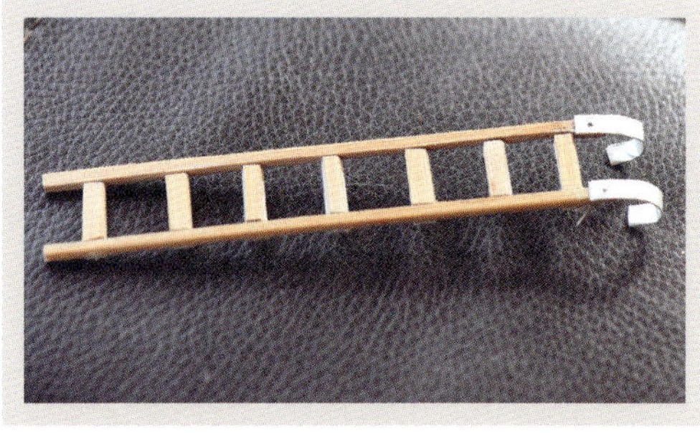

5 | The straight ladder made of wooden slats extends with hooks made from twist ties. Two small cut pins serve as nails.

6 | For windows, two evening landscapes were cut from a magazine and covered with pill blister packaging to create a glass effect, then framed in black paper. These will be glued to the head of the bed. The blinds are made from rectangles of black fabric, with two pins inserted into the top hem to act as curtain rods, glued to a small piece of black cardboard, and a wire ring is sewn at the bottom. You can leave one blind open and pull the other down.

7 | The curtains are sewn from thin white nonwoven fabric, pleated, and tied with a thin ribbon. Jump rings are sewn onto the top hem and slide along the curtain rod, which is made from a skewer covered in copper adhesive tape.

8 | The sleeping bags and pillows are made from patterned cotton fabric, filled with fleece or batting for thickness. Sew them inside out, turn them right-side out, and finish the seams by hand.

The Corner Bathroom

9 | To make the fake round mirror, cut the bottom of a soda can with a craft knife and refine the cut with scissors.

10 | The small wall cabinet is made from a vintage metal box. To add shelves, cut a rectangle of metal from the soda can, fold it to make two shelves, glue the folds, then glue the entire piece to the bottom of the box.

11 | Cut a piece of cardboard to the size of the suitcase lid. Cover it with patterned paper. Attach all the elements to it: this will be glued to the suitcase lid at the very end, after the lighting is added (the wires from the light string will be hidden behind, and it will be perforated so that two LED bulbs point under the wall sconces). Glue wooden slats cut from a crate to the floor.

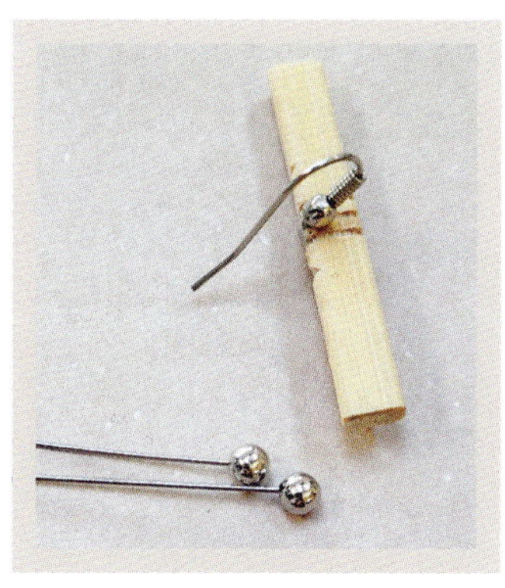

12 | To make the faucet, use the curved stem of an earring attached to a bamboo section from a chopstick, and create two small notches to hold the silver beads from two sewing pins.

16 | The small trash can is a cut section of a marker. A button serves as the lid, with a wire handle. Another wire, heated over a candle, is pushed in to act as the pedal.

13 | For the basin, choose an appropriate seashell and glue it to the wooden frame. A smaller shell can serve as the soap dish. The soap can be taken from a piece of eraser or shaped from a few drops of warm wax.

17 | The wooden shelves under the sink are cut from a small disposable spoon. Once all these elements are made, arrange them, then glue them in place while ensuring that the suitcase can still be closed.

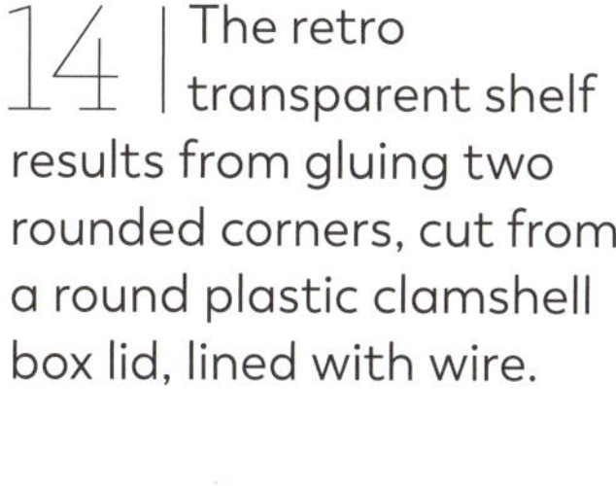

14 | The retro transparent shelf results from gluing two rounded corners, cut from a round plastic clamshell box lid, lined with wire.

15 | A broken ballpoint pen was used to cut a translucent toothbrush holder, while its metal tip, adorned with a pinhead, acts as a bottle. In the wall cabinet, two other bottles are made from pen sections with lids made of buttons, and two narrower ones come from the ink tube of the same pen, with a bead as the stopper. Variations are pictured below.

Small Decorative Elements

18 | To make the sconces, bend a pearl-headed pin and thread two flower-shaped beads onto it.

19 | The towel holder is made from a paper clip, with a nonwoven towel, and beads glued to the ends.

22 | Pattern for the tissue box.

20 | Here is the pattern to make a small toiletry bag from textured paper, with a cord zipper.

21 | The glasses are made from thin flexible wire, wrapped around a pencil to make the round shapes.

23 | Simply bend a paper clip to make a clever hanger (see page 106).

The Accessories

24 | The small camera is made from balsa wood. The lens is the metal eraser tip of a pencil, with the eraser painted black and a metal ring glued to it.

25 | Make a felt hat by tying a circle over a bottle cap. The striped pajama top is folded and glued to cardboard.

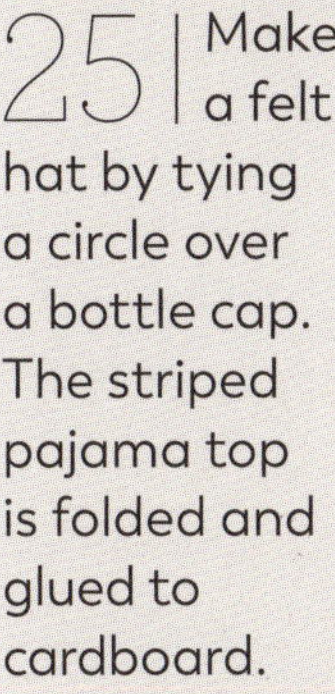

26 | Here is the pattern for the two small bathrobes made from microfiber towels, folded in half without hems, with an added pocket and a thin ribbon belt.

27 | The dwarf slippers are easy to make as long as you find the right fabric (here, red fleece and suede).

The Luggage

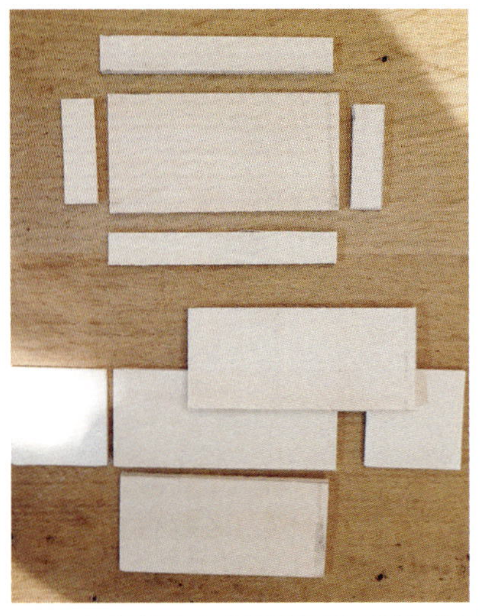

28 | To make the small trunk, cut pieces of balsa wood according to the pattern above to create two boxes. Cover them with fabric after placing batting on the lid. Add copper tape corners, a lock salvaged from a cigar box, miniature buckles, and small printed travel tags.

29 | A vanity case is made from the cap of a shampoo bottle (with a handle and a bead glued on), and a small bag is made from a binder clip.

30 | The suitcase is a matchbox covered with marbled paper taken from the front page of an old book. The fake nails are very tiny pins. Unlike the trunk, this does not open.

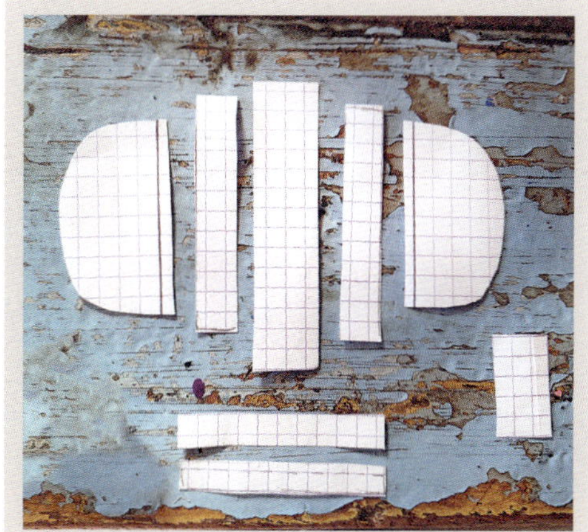

31 | The pattern for the bag made from beige imitation suede, to be sewn by hand. The strips at the bottom form the handles. The pocket is on the lower right. The small rolled-up newspaper inside is a label.

32 | A cardboard bag covered with plaid paper. The gusset sides are folded into triangles and then glued. The cord handles and the closing elastic loop are threaded through the cardboard and glued inside.

33 | Behind the ladder, hiding the light switch is a fabric bag stuffed with batting and with a mini tag.

34 | Run the LED light string on the left, under the wall lights (drill two holes) and all around the inner edge; on the right, above the beds. Then glue on the bathroom panel.

THE SPELUNKERS' CAVE

MATERIALS

structure: three thick books of the same size (to sacrifice)

—

lighting: thin, short string of LED lights with button cell batteries

—

to repurpose: small plastic soldiers with weapons removed, mini clockwork mechanism

—

small materials: colored cord, matches, fine gravel, small pebbles, moss, green tissue paper, adhesive tape

—

tools: jigsaw, clamp, drill with straight and winged bits, small rotary tool with a circular saw, file, craft knife, scissors, hot glue gun

Sculpting the Cave

DO SOMETHING RADICAL: DIG INTO THE MATERIAL OF THE BOOK AND EXPLORE ITS DEPTHS . . . LITERALLY!

1 | Trace the most open shape of the cave on one of the books and cut it with a jigsaw at an inclined angle, ensuring it is securely held in a clamp. This will be the middle book.

2 | Transfer the shape onto the other two books and cut only the cover touching the middle book on each. The rest will be done with a craft knife. Carve slopes into the bottom book, forming a lake at the base.

3 | Refine the shape with the craft knife, erode the edges, and create curves like contour lines. Damage the sides with a file or abrasive disk. Leave a recess in the vault for the lighting.

4 | Drill into the thickness of the top book with a drill to create a hole large enough for a crouching soldier and extend this hole into a gallery by carving with the circular blade of a rotary tool.

5 | Drill the first cover of the top book with an auger bit to create a kind of well. File the edges to create irregularities in the walls. Apply glue around the area and add gravel, small pebbles, and bits of moss. Glue three matchsticks in a tepee shape above the opening, as well as a colored cord wrapped around a small watch gear.

Adding the Details

6 | Tie one end of the cord around a soldier and have him hold it in place of his rifle. Thread the rest of the cord into the hole, glue a crawling soldier (when vertical, he becomes climbing) inside the hole, and secure the other end of the cord with another soldier on the ground inside the cave. The last two soldiers will be glued in the front gallery, disarmed.

7 | Form stalactites drop by drop with a candle and glue them to the cave ceiling.

8 | Line the bottom of the lake with green tissue paper and glue five LEDs underneath. The string of lights continues through a hole in the ceiling, then behind the soldiers in the front gallery.

THE HACIENDA

MATERIALS

box: ¼-inch (6-mm) MDF board

—

lighting: thin string of LED lights with button cell batteries

—

essential to find: wooden perforated fan, dangling earrings

—

to repurpose: skewers, stir sticks, craft sticks, bottom of a cigar box, pendant shaped like a mini key, pull tab from a can, small plant sprigs

—

craft materials: natural clay, plaster, air-dry clay, tissue paper in a variety of colors

—

small materials: twine, thin wire, light wood beads, flat glass bead, glue, pins, cloth, paint, wax, sandpaper

—

tools: saw, hammer, hole punchers (for holes and patterns), craft knife, scissors, pliers, drill, file, spatula

The Fan Staircase

A SMALL COURTYARD WITH AUTHENTIC FINISHES, UNDER A STRING OF MEXICAN PENNANTS. THE CENTRAL IDEA: SHOWCASING A BEAUTIFUL SPIRAL STAIRCASE MADE FROM A FAN, WHICH IS EASIER TO MAKE THAN IT SEEMS.

1 | Disassemble the fan and carefully cut it with small scissors to obtain steps of the desired size: one end will encompass the solid wood bulge and the other will contour the curved design of the motif.

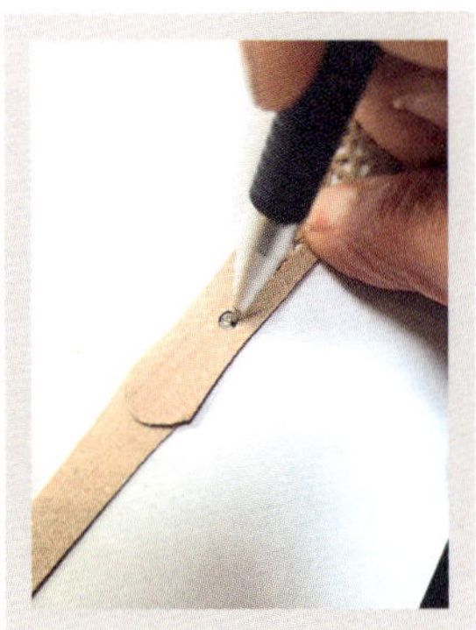

2 | Punch a hole in each strip (either before or after cutting) and transfer the hole to the next strip to ensure that they are all properly aligned.

3 | Cut stir sticks and glue them along the designs on one edge to form the risers.

4 | Choose wooden beads of the same thickness as the stir sticks (¼ inch or 5 mm) and with a hole large enough for a skewer to pass through. If necessary, thin the skewer slightly with sandpaper. Thread the steps onto the skewer, alternating with beads and leaving the skewer to protrude at both the top and the bottom. The height of the skewer will be adjusted at the end. It is easier if you insert the skewer into a support, such as a small piece of polystyrene. Adjust the steps as needed to give the staircase a regular shape, then glue them in place. The number of steps determines the height of the floor. In this case, we have chosen a slight diagonal start for a landing that runs parallel to the sidewall, which corresponds to seventeen steps.

The Landing and the Handrail

5 | Make the landing using craft sticks.

6 | Braid three strands of twine around a wire. This thin flexible braid will serve as the handrail.

7 | Glue wooden skewers vertically on every fourth step, extending 1¼ inches (3 cm) above the step. Keep the main skewer of the staircase longer. Connect these posts with a railing made of kitchen twine, wrapping it around the posts on two levels, then glue the braided handrail on top.

8 | Use leftover pieces from the fan to create the two handrails for the landing. The decorative elements are sandwiched at the bottom between two slats, and at the top between two chopsticks, topped with a flat stick.

9 | Make a hole in the base of the box to insert the central skewer.

The Door and the Window

10 | To make the door and its frame, use the bottom of a cigar box, as it is made from fine veneer wood that is slightly darker than the staircase. Glue the door and doorframe onto a white paper rectangle that shows through the fan scraps placed where the windows would be.

11 | The handle is a small piece of twisted wire. The entire piece is self-contained, glued with wood glue, and ready to be attached to the wall.

12 | The trapezoidal shape of the fan scraps makes it easy to create this window inspired by mashrabiyas. The window is assembled by gluing the scraps onto a foam board base reinforced with small sticks at the back.

The Walls

13 | Mix a few tablespoons of plaster with water until you get a smooth paste. Wet one of the walls, then quickly spread the plaster (it hardens quickly) with a painter's knife or spatula, without trying to make it even; on the contrary, cover the entire surface unevenly.

14 | Immediately add blue pigments or paint and spread it with the knife. Once dry, apply a very diluted black wash with a brush, rubbing, scraping, wearing down, and staining the surface as desired. The plaster base makes it easy to achieve a rough look. Proceed in this way for the back wall and the left wall. The right wall will remain in white plaster.

15 | As a final step, use a cloth to apply wax, oil, or glycerin to intensify the color.

The Floor

16 | To make the tiled floor, mix plaster with natural clay dissolved in water.

17 | Spread it on the floor with a knife in a somewhat thick layer (about 1⁄16 inch or 2 mm).

18 | Mark a grid with a ruler before the mixture has fully dried.

19 | Soften the edges by running a round-tipped tool around each square.

21 | Since the washes are fragile on this crumbly surface, it is easy to create a worn appearance by rubbing with a cloth and a bit of wax.

20 | Apply one or more coats of diluted paint the color of the tiles using a brush, being careful not to go into the crevices in order to keep them visible.

22 | Glue down the staircase, the door, the key next to it, and the window.

The Sconce

23 | The wall sconce on the right is cut from the lid of a can with a pull tab.

24 | Glue the flat part to the wall and twist the ring to make it horizontal. Hang colorful earrings that evoke Latin America and cover the circle with a flat glass bead.

25 | The light string will be threaded through the smallest hole and the light will shine through the glass bead.

The Accessories

26 | Create a large flowerpot by gluing scraps of the fan onto four matchsticks that serve as supports at the corners and extend to form the legs.

27 | Place a bouquet of small dried feathers inside, evoking the tall grasses of the Pampas.

28 | You can also have fun creating a small bench, using the leftover fan pieces, some wood strips, and matchsticks. To ensure symmetry in the pattern, two pieces have been joined together to form the backrest.

The Flowerpots

29 | Stick pine branches in a cork.

30 | Insert boxwood into a small painted clay pot.

31 | Arrange dried alder cones, painted green, in a painted wooden bead pot.

32 | Shape cacti from air-dry clay and paint them, or make cacti from colored modeling clay.

33 | Make a plant by gluing two strips of green tissue paper, in various shades, onto one or two fine wires, then shape them into points and assemble them in a clay pot covering a cork.

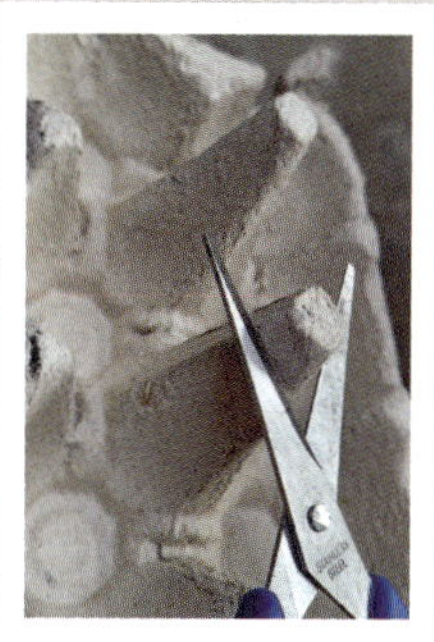

34 | You can also create cute little raw pots by cutting off the inner tips of an egg carton.

The String of Lights

35 | Punch holes in various colored tissue paper pieces using different decorative hole punches. Cut them into pennants and glue them onto the LED garland to imitate the *papel picado* from Mexican celebrations. Leave three LED bulbs closest to the case as is.

36 | Hang the end of the garland in the front-left corner, stretch it above the door, leaving some slack at the ceiling so it lights up the center without blocking the window. Attach another fixing point (using glue) in the top-right corner of the window, then curve it along the white wall to the wall sconce. At this point, twist three LED bulbs under the flat glass bead, then glue the battery case under the ceiling on the right, hidden behind some small fan scraps glued in place.

First published in the United States of America in 2026 by
Rizzoli Universe, a Division of
Rizzoli International Publications, Inc.
49 West 27th Street
New York, NY 10001
rizzoliusa.com

Originally published in French in 2024 as *La magie des Book Nooks : Créations miniatures à glisser dans sa bibliothèque* by Editions Gallimard, collection Hoëbeke, Paris, France
gallimard.fr

For Rizzoli
Publisher: Charles Miers
Editor: Klaus Kirschbaum
Assistant Editor: Emily Ligniti
Managing Editor: Lynn Scrabis
Translator: Christiana Hills

ISBN: 978-0-7893-4618-6
Library of Congress Control Number: 2025947645

Printed in Slovenia
2026 2027 2028 / 10 9 8 7 6 5 4 3 2 1

The authorized representative in the EU for product safety and compliance is
Mondadori Libri S.p.A., via Gian Battista Vico 42,
Milan, Italy, 20123
mondadori.it

Visit us online
Facebook.com/RizzoliNewYork
Instagram.com/RizzoliBooks
Youtube.com/user/RizzoliNY

Would you like to learn how to make book nooks? I organize themed stays at my home in theAlpes-de-Haute-Provence, combining holidays in an idyllic setting with creative workshops. . . .

raphaelevidaling.fr
@raphaelevidaling

ACKNOWLEDGMENTS

First of all, I would like to thank my mother, who passed on to me the love of crafting with my hands and the patience to devote countless hours to it. She created the sleeper car, the buildings on the street, the bakery window, the cabin that I perched above the water, the stairs and decor of the hacienda, as well as the artist's studio and all its accessories.

Thanks to Diana, who helped me considerably with the creation of the kitchen, bakery, and library (she made the armchair, chandelier, fireplace, and lots of books).

Thanks to Léo, who designed the spiral of scribbles (Instagram @GrisBouillis), and to Pauline, who created the paper landscape inspired by fairy tales (website: pauline-cottereau-junker.ultra-book.com).

Thanks to Max, who built boxes and bravely sawed the books for the flea market and cave, and to Guillaume, who finalized the spelunking cave, created the little fawn's magical cave, and supported me daily.